# The Pursuit of Revival

# The Pursuit of Revival

## Stephen Hill

CREATION
HOUSE
Orlando, FL

THE PURSUIT OF REVIVAL by Stephen Hill
Published by Creation House
Strang Communications Company
600 Rinehart Road
Lake Mary, Florida 32746
Web site: http://www.creationhouse.com

Unless otherwise noted, all Scripture quotations are from the King James Version of the Bible.

Scripture quotations marked NAS are from the New American Standard Bible. Copyright © 1960, 1962, 1963, 1968, 1971, 1972, 1973, 1975, 1977 by the Lockman Foundation. Used by permission.

*Printed in the United States of America*
Library of Congress Catalog Card Number: 97-06835
ISBN:0-88419-506-6
78901234 BBG 87654321

To HUGH MOZINGO, the dear Lutheran vicar who took the time on October 28, 1975, to lead me to Jesus.

Thank you, Brother, for not giving up on someone whom most people thought would die in his sins.

May the Lord richly reward you!

# Acknowledgments

SPECIAL THANKS TO Jo Kadlecek for your editorial assistance and writing skills. In the midst of revival, you have helped us record the events—as they happened. Your love for Jesus and burden for souls made working together a pleasure. God bless you.

Also, please allow me to get just a little sentimental. On this page, I want to express my deep love to my older sister, Marcia Pate, my older brother, George Hill, and my younger sister, Susan Hill, for their love and support throughout the years. You're the best brother and sisters on the planet. I love you.

# Contents

# Foreword

**M**ORNINGS WERE the worst. Waking up at noon with a pounding hangover after another eighteen-hour drug binge was normal for me. I was doing acid, cocaine, pot, and lots of beer. I tried to live "high," but I always ended up coming down. *Why am I doing this?* I thought. *I don't want to do these drugs. I don't even like these people I am with.* But the mornings: the headaches, the pain, the memory . . . *Oh well, I'll just smoke a joint and it will all go away.* Regret was my way of life for two-and-a-half years, morning by morning.

At one time I was a fun-loving Florida teenager. I had a

good childhood and a good home even though my parents divorced when I was young. My dad took me to church every Sunday, and I thought of myself as a good Christian kid. I had dreams and goals like most teenagers. I wanted to go to college, join the military, and ultimately work with the DEA as a drug-control agent.

Those goals all vanished when I ended up on the opposite side of my dream. I was kicked out of the house when I was nineteen because I had been fired from my job. I worked another job, but was fired from that also. I had friends who were bartending and bouncing for bars, so I hung out with them. One night, I busted up a big fight and was offered my first job as a bouncer.

From there, I moved up to bigger and more popular bars. I discovered that I could hurt people, and I actually learned to enjoy it. I liked to pound people in their temples and watch their eyes roll back into their head. I would head-butt people in the face over a two-dollar cover charge. I became mean, cruel, and violent. I was evil and full of hate.

All of this took time, morning by morning. It didn't happen overnight. But by the time I was twenty-two I began to smoke marijuana—a lot of it. Everyday, every night. Like I said, I tried to live "high." I began selling pot to make a little money on the side.

People who say pot doesn't lead to other drugs are so wrong. Doing pot introduced me to people that were involved in harder drugs. Soon, I began to mix and experiment with these other drugs. It was a downward spiral that never stopped: Pot, acid, cocaine.

Finally, a Cuban friend of mine approached me in wintertime. Things were slow in Destin, Florida, so his offer to make some serious money was irresistible. I started to sell harder drugs in serious quantities. I began to make trips to Miami, Texas, and the Florida Keys to get drugs. I was getting in deep. All the time, I was becoming harder and harder.

In the spring of 1996, I reached an all-time low. I had been stiffed on a deal in Texas and had lost several hundred dollars which I had borrowed from Dad. I was afraid to talk to him, so I didn't call or anything. I just sort of disappeared for a while. Suddenly, I was more alone than I had ever been. I didn't have any real friends. I hated my life, and now I had lost my relationship with my dad, my best friend.

Somehow, I ended up at my sister's house in Alabama. A Christian, she convinced me to call my dad after two months of silence. I called him the morning of June 1. I didn't know it at the time, but that was the last morning I was ever going to feel alone, evil, or empty. Dad told me about a revival going on in Pensacola and asked if I wanted to go. *Sure, why not?* I thought.

When I walked into Brownsville Assembly of God, I felt a little out of place. Standing six foot four and weighing 285 pounds is one thing. Having a goatee and shoulder length hair done up in braids and pulled back into a fat ponytail was something else. I tried to look tough and intimidating, but inside I wanted to hide, so we sat in the balcony. God was dealing with my heart, and He didn't let up through the whole service. I felt like God was after me, pursuing me. I couldn't understand why, but all I could do was cry during the whole service. Of course, I wiped away every tear before anybody could see it.

The people in the revival seemed so alive. The music was beautiful. I told my dad it sounded like angels singing. Suddenly, everything changed and a Presence entered the room. It was heavy and deep. People began to weep and cry out to God. Steve Hill began calling people to the altar. I kept telling myself and even my dad that I was okay, I had made my peace with God. I knew I was lying. I knew that He was trying to get hold of me.

Steve Hill then pointed up to the balcony where I was sitting and said, "God knows about your drug problem." At the very last moment before the altar call was closed, I broke. I couldn't fight God anymore, and I couldn't take the pain and the stress of my life anymore. I went down to the altar, crying openly the whole way. I fell on my face before God and poured out my heart to Him. "God, I can't take it anymore! I hate this evil life, and I can't take the burden. Please take it all out of my heart. I need You, Jesus." Instantly, I felt the evil leave me. I felt the burden lift as the stress was covered in peace. I was finally free!

When I woke up the next morning, I still had the peace. I didn't have any regret and the pain was gone. I was brand new in Jesus! He had washed away all the junk from my life. I knew what it meant to be in Christ and to be a new creature. The old things had really passed away, and all things were brand new. Three weeks later, I was baptized at Brownsville and I have been on fire ever since.

These days, I pursue God. I'm in revival every night. God has given me a desire for Him like nothing I have ever had before. Like Adam in the garden, I live in fellowship with God, walking in the cool of the day with my Father. Now I'm not trying to get high all the time. I live with a joy that no drug could ever give me. In fact, I have now been clean for over a year, and I have no desire to go back to that way of life. I couldn't—I just couldn't go back.

God has put a love in my heart for people that is more intense than the hate and violence that I used to have. Now I walk around with a smile on my face ready to give a hug to anyone. I told God one morning, "I don't want to hurt anyone ever again." I have entered the Brownsville Revival School of Ministry so that I can be better equipped to work with young people who are going through the same things I went through. I want to see people go after God, and I want to help them.

Now, mornings are different. I love to watch the sun rise and spend time with Jesus. I'm still up late a lot these days, but it's spending time with Jesus, worshiping Him. The people I'm with these days are full of God, and I love to be with them. People like Steve Hill. I'm doing what God wants me to do. The best part is waking up and knowing that Jesus is with me, and He has an awesome plan for each day. Peace is my way of life now, and God's mercy is new every morning. I have one goal in my life now—to know Jesus more intimately.

In this book, *The Pursuit of Revival,* you will read about the Brownsville Revival. You will understand more about the passion of the evangelist, and read first-hand accounts of how the power of God is changing lives. Pastor John Kilpatrick, Stephen Hill, Michael Brown, Lindell Cooley, and the rest of the ministry staff are in constant pursuit of God. They live with the daily expectation that Jesus Christ is going to do more than they could possibly imagine. They are in pursuit of revival!

—*Patrick Waters*
*A sinner saved by Grace*

# Preface

THROUGHOUT world history, there have been special seasons of grace where God Almighty chose to pour out His Spirit upon the land. Sometimes these outpourings lasted only a few days—but dealt a powerful death blow to the devil. Other times, these sweet visitations would go on for months, even years, soaking a people in His blessed presence.

These marvelous moments of mercy were usually preceded by a long season of spiritual drought. The church was at an all-time low in spiritual power and numerical attendance. The country as a whole had been drifting down a path of sin and degradation. They had lost the grip of God's hand and were being led away by the powers of darkness. Evil practices, occultic worship, love of pleasure, life-controlling vices such as alcohol consumption and sexual lust were rampant. Rivalry and fights, a disregard for the warnings in God's Word, a disdain for truth, an unconcern for holiness, and a hellish philosophy of "eat, drink, and be merry, for tomorrow we die" were often the rule of the day.

But somewhere in the country, off on a hillside in a small cottage littered within by a few pieces of humble furniture, off in a corner, you would find a small two-foot-by-four-foot braided rug—and on that rug would be worn-out spots where somebody, some dear saint of God, had knelt praying day after day, night after night. Laboring like a mother would labor in giving birth, these saints prayed for a spiritual awakening in their country. Amid all the smoke of hell outside, inside that little cottage was the clean air of heaven.

There have always been pockets of believers, sprinkled throughout the land—earnestly seeking God—motivated by a desperate desire for revival. God has always had His remnant. They took hold of the horns of the altar. The darkness of night was pierced by their agonizing pleas for a visitation from God. Their white-hot prayers lit up the sky just as lightning displaces utter blackness.

As barrooms and dance halls would be seen full of sinners two-steppin' with the devil, just a few doors down in a small apartment would be a dear saint of God pounding the tongue-and-groove pinewood floor with his fists, blasting out fiery arrows of intercession—such as John Knox's haunting words, "Give me Scotland, or I die." The hierarchy during his time went down in history as saying, "I am more afraid of John Knox's prayers than I am of all the armies of the world."

The corridors of heaven would ring with the consistent, dogmatic, God-demanding, heartfelt, soul-stirring, tear-drenched, insistent, persistent, un-ceasing, unwavering, crystal-clear cries for mercy.

Before long, the faithfulness of God would reign supreme. Just as God answered the bellowing cries of Brownsville for revival, over the centuries He has faithfully turned His ear toward the prayer warrior. He has always been moved by the Christian warrior's zeal and his intense concern for the welfare of mankind. I can imagine Him standing up in the throne room of heaven, raising His right hand and saying, "Gabriel, sound the war cry, gather ten thousand of our seasoned war angels. Holy Spirit—the time has come. Jesus, My Son, it is time. May you now receive reward for Your suffering. Holy Ghost, flood that nation with Your Presence!"

I can hear the Father say, "See that band of believers? Yes, that one hundred twenty in the upper room. I unleash the power of heaven. Tongues of fire—fall! Mighty wind—blow! Fill them with power—Now! Anoint them! Consume them! Revival now!" I can hear the Lord say, "They're gathering together at Cane Ridge. Thousands are craving a touch from Me. Drench those hungry souls in Kentucky with rain from Heaven." The orders continue: "Armies of Heaven, join ranks with Evan Roberts. His prayers have been answered. Sweep through Wales. Melt the hearts of the coal-miners. May their coal-dust covered faces be streaked with tracks of repentant tears."

I can hear the cry at the turn of this century, "Holy Spirit, fall in that little shack on Azusa Street! Touch, Holy Spirit, our dear brother Seymour. Flood every hungry heart. Baptize them with fire!"

"Wesley, Whitefield, Tennent, Edwards, Brainerd, Finney—take *this* from the storehouse of heaven! Receive the anointing, and preach My Word to the masses!"

These soldiers who went before us were in the constant pursuit of revival. God heard their cry and answered their prayers. Determine in your heart to be one of those who won't flinch in the heat of battle. Go after God with unquenchable zeal. Be a Wesley, be an Edwards, be a Finney: Be in pursuit of revival.

—*STEPHEN HILL*
*PENSACOLA, FLORIDA*

# Introduction

UPON RETURNING to the United States in February, my wife Ruth and I visited Pensacola, Florida, accompanied by a small group of friends. We went to attend the meetings at Brownsville Assembly of God, concerning which reports have gone out widely that there is revival in progress. Our group consisted of three couples, all in full-time ministry, and a single sister. We were able to attend three nights of meetings (Tuesday, Wednesday, and Thursday), so my report is only based on the meetings at which I was present.

Tuesday night was prayer meeting. It was the only

meeting we could get into without waiting in line. The seventeen hundred people present represented quite a large turn-out by most standards of prayer meetings. Further, it was a very "mobile" prayer meeting. In the course of the evening, we went to every single area of the church building, including restrooms, Sunday school rooms, passages, and entrances. The purpose was to drive out all demonic influences and spirits—and there was a very wholehearted assault made on them by all the people there. Interestingly, there was no singing; they just went straight into prayer.

One distinctive feature was the presence of ten or more banners, each one representing some major theme of prayer. People focused their prayer on a theme by gathering around that particular banner. There was, therefore, none of what I would call "shotgun praying" rather, it was very directed. Nearing the end of the meeting, prayer was further directed toward the four regions: North, South, East, and West. The "Warfare" and "Souls" banners were carried to each corresponding side of the sanctuary. At that point, I found myself praying especially toward the south which from Pensacola, is Latin America, where I had recently ministered. While praying for Latin America, I had a powerful physical manifestation in my own body, which seemed to me to indicate that area is a place God has on His list for me.

Then, on Wednesday and Thursday nights, the meetings were evangelistic. They opened with powerful congregational worship which lasted quite a long while. The building was filled to capacity, as were two other large buildings apart from the main sanctuary. The pastor was John Kilpatrick and the evangelist, Stephen Hill. We enjoyed a little time of fellowship with them both. In speaking to Stephen, I recall saying to him, "I think you're the only preacher I know who quotes more scriptures than I do." The emphasis of the ministry focused on two things: repentance and holiness. It was when I became aware of this emphasis that I made up my mind—*Pensacola is the place I want to be.*

Steve Hill didn't deal with sin in just a general way. He dealt with and described very specific sins. I think the sin that was most focused on while we were there was pornography. When I saw the response of the people, I realized how widespread this sin is, even among professing Christians. On the first night, the appeal was first and foremost for backslidden leaders and about two hundred came forward. Then, there was a more general appeal and about four hundred made their way to the crowded altar. On Thursday, the appeal was a little more general and again at least four hundred people came forward. Each night, all were individually counseled.

One thing my wife, Ruth, appreciated so tremendously was that the evangelist called backsliders to come back to the Lord. She said, "He wasn't talking about people who were totally out of the church, but people who were not living their lives 100 percent in consciousness that Jesus was watching every move they made. He talked about things like watching the wrong television programs, listening to bad language and not even being offended by it, letting people take the name of the Lord in vain in your presence and not objecting. I grieve for the church of Jesus Christ because there are so many people who believe that they are on their way to heaven, when they are actually sliding backward, little by little—day by day—and do not even know it. That is why I am so grateful to hear that kind of preaching in America."

There were a good many people slain in the Spirit, and I noticed a few other manifestations, but nothing that I would call particularly dramatic or striking. Nothing, at any rate, that in any way offended me. I felt that everybody on the whole team of the church—both the official ministers and the lay people—were genuinely, deeply concerned for the well-being of those to whom they had ministered. I watched the faces of one or two prayer-team members as they prayed for those who had come forward, and I saw such genuine compassion on their faces. I would say the general atmosphere was "free," but nevertheless under authority. You didn't feel that anything could break loose that wouldn't be in some way dealt with. The staff were amazingly friendly and accessible in view of all the responsibilities that they had. The other members, the lay members, were usually up past midnight in the meeting and then at work next morning. They were committed people; I didn't see any focus on human personality.

Interestingly, there were two Messianic Jews on the teaching staff, one of them a long-time friend of ours. I think that this perhaps is a very significant symptom, because I have come to the conclusion that the church worldwide can never be what God intended it to be until the Jews take their rightful place again in the church. I see this happening in a dramatic way. In fact, it has been happening ever since Israel recovered the Old City and the Temple Mount in 1967. That somehow seemed to accelerate the in gathering of Jewish people worldwide. There are now hundreds of thousands of Jewish believers all over the globe.

It would be natural for people to ask, "Well, what was the impact of the revival?" I'll just mention a few points which are by no means intended to be comprehensive. Every day when there was an evangelistic service scheduled, people would begin lining up about 5:00 A.M., to get into a meeting that started at 7:00 P.M. Now, that is unusual, to make the most modest comment. Anywhere people are lining up for more than twelve hours to get into a church service, something unusual is happening!

Then again, the whole community in Pensacola in conscious of what is taking place. It happened that one of our party phoned a motel to ask how far it was located from the church. The person phoning never had to say anything more than "the church," and immediately the person at the motel knew that it was Brownsville Assembly of God. As far as Pensacola is concerned, Brownsville is "the Church."

Incidentally, the economic situation of the town has gone up considerably. The local city council attribute the growth to their efforts; but I think it has got more to do with God than with them. Another delightful statistic: Last year (1996), the juvenile crime rate in Florida as a state went up 1 percent. In the county in which Brownsville Assembly of God is located, however, it went *down* 13 percent. Before the revival began, there were only three student Christian groups in area school—now, there are thirty-two!

There was another very interesting thing that impressed all of our party at the prayer meeting on Tuesday night. We were asked to pray that there would be an "open heaven" the following nights over Pensacola. My wife and I usually read our Bible together in the mornings, and the following morning we did so. I said to Ruth, "It is amazing how much we are getting out of the Bible this morning. I am seeing things I never saw before." When we shared this with the other members in our party, they all said virtually the same thing. So, I conclude, that means when there is an open heaven, communication with God is easier and more profitable.

Now let me just say a little bit about the background,

the roots of this revival—I think revival is a fair word to use. Several years of prayer for revival have taken place in that particular congregation, led by the pastor who also has a personal burden for revival. At some point, Pastor Kilpatrick felt led to change the Sunday evening service to a prayer meeting. He was very concerned that his congregation would dwindle, but in actual fact, it increased. We also heard that of the original congregation, 80 percent of them were regular tithers. Of course, that agrees with the promise found in Malachi 3:10: "Bring ye all the tithes into the storehouse, that there may be meat in mine house, and prove me now herewith, saith the Lord of hosts, if I will not open you the windows of heaven, and pour you out a blessing, that there shall not be room enough to receive it." What we do with our finances has a lot to do with the spiritual consequences we experience.

I saw, in the leadership there, a willingness to make room for the Holy Spirit. Even though some of the manifestations that came were very unexpected, unusual, and could be interpreted as somewhat undignified—nevertheless, they yielded to the Holy Spirit. Jesus was central, there was no focus on any human personality. He was the Alpha and Omega—it all revolved around Him.

What I am about to point out is possibly the most important element in this brief overview of the situation in Pensacola, and what led up to the revival. I conclude that the congregation at Brownsville did not do anything that all other Christians can not do. In other words, everything they did was something that all Christians could do if they set their minds to it. It was Charles Finney who said that revival is not an accident anymore than a crop of wheat is an accident. If you plant the right seed and care for the crop while it's growing, you will get a revival. I think Finney was right.

There is another scripture that comes to my mind in connection with this—Jeremiah 8:20: "The harvest is past, the summer is ended, and we are not saved." A kind of grief comes over me as I utter those words. How tragic for people to have been there at the "time of the harvest," yet at the end, they still "are not saved." My own prayer for myself and our ministry is that we will never be responsible, by lack of diligence and commitment, for causing people to say, "We are not saved." As far as I am concerned this is the Harvest Hour all over the world. My wife and I are committed to doing our utmost to make sure nobody says at the end, "The harvest is past, the summer is ended, and we are not saved." Oh, how tragic! How tragic!

I must relate something here that occurred recently in our local church in Fort Lauderdale. A Bulgarian evangelist was there, a man with a very sweet spirit who had obviously experienced a recent encounter with the Lord. I asked him to pray for me. I told him, "I have invested a lot in Bulgaria; a lot of my material is there and I would like for you to pray for me."

He responded, "You are my teacher. How can I pray for you?" But he did so, and I found myself kneeling under the power of God.

During that night and into Monday morning I was awake, and I had a number of very powerful impressions. First of all, I felt I was listening to what I would call an inaudible cry of thousands upon thousands of people in a particular area of Florida (Fort Lauderdale). Their mass cry was somehow summed up in these words:

*"I am replaceable; nobody really cares about me." "If I were to drown, there would be a little ripple on the surface of the water, but no one would dive in to save me."*

*"I may be working in an office, a factory, or a store, and I get my pay and my two weeks holiday, but if I did not show up, in a few weeks nobody would even remember me." "I am replaceable."*

I thought about the words of David from one of the Psalms: "No man cared for my soul" (Ps. 142:4). As I felt the cry from this multitude, I had a feeling of unbearable pain. I felt such pain that if I had been under it for more than a second, it would have crushed the life out of me. I believe it was the pain of those people who felt that no one cared for them. Then, suddenly, I began to have a little sense of the pain God feels for these people. I realized in a totally new dimension that God loves the world. He loves every soul that has ever been created, and He longs for each one individually. The Lord grieves and agonizes over every soul that does not return to Him.

I trust that will be an inspiration and a blessing to you. At least it has given me a somewhat new perspective on what the ministry is, and what the message of the gospel is. I want to be able to assure people: "God cares for you, and *we* care for you."

—Reverend Derek Prince
*Excerpt from his personal Update #82*
*Recorded April 1997*

# William Jenkyn on Revivals

*(an English Pastor from the 1600s)*

A REVIVAL IS THE SPRING of Christianity—the
renovation of life and gladness.

It is the season in which young converts
   burst into existence and beautiful activity.
The Church resumes her toil, labor and care
   with freshness and energy.
The air all around is balmy, and
   diffusing the sweetest aromas.
The whole landscape teems with living promises
   of abundant harvest of righteousness and peace.

It is the jubilee of holiness.
A pleasant warmth pervades and
   refreshes the whole Church.
Showers of "heavenly delight and joy" descend
   gently and lavishly.
A delightful atmosphere is carried on every breeze.

Where the dead leaves of winter still linger,
   the primrose and the daisy spring up
      in modest loveliness.
Trees long barren put forth the buds
   of beauty and power.
The whole valley is crowned with
   fragrant and varied blossoms.
Forms of beauty bloom on every side,
   and Zion is the joy of the whole earth.

If the spirit that renews the face of the earth
   is a spirit of beauty . . .
      in the elegance of the inception,
the tints of the buds, the richness of the foliage,
   the splendor of the blossoms and
      the alluring glories
of the matured fruits of Nature . . .
   "how great is His beauty" when acting out His
      lovely and holy perfections in revivals of
   Christianity.

*Chapter One*

# The Great Calamity

*For though I preach the gospel, I have nothing to glory of: for necessity is laid upon me; yea, woe is unto me, if I preach not the gospel!*

—1 CORINTHIANS 9:16

A T THE TIME of this writing, we are entering the third year of a remarkable revival at Brownsville Assembly of God in Pensacola, Florida. Those of us who have been a part of this mighty move of God have prayed throughout our Christian lives for revival. But few of us really expected to see it with our own eyes. What has become known as the Father's Day Outpouring took all of us by surprise.

Maybe it shouldn't have. When we consider the wonders of God Almighty, the One who called many of us out of some dark and desperate world, an outpouring of this

1

magnitude should be anything but surprising. Still, we are limited by our human experiences and so a revival like the kind we read about in church history seemed, well, unlikely in the 1990s.

The Holy Spirit, however, has a way of changing everything, especially when people begin to pray. Through prayer, we have watched the power of the risen Lord Jesus soften even the hardest of hearts. Through prayer, we have felt the healing touch of the Savior renew and refresh our own spirits. Through prayer, we have watched in awe, night after night in revival services, as the King of kings has proclaimed His lordship over more than one hundred thousand new converts and backsliders as they come to the altar broken by their sin. Countless lives have been changed as a result of this revival.

I, for one, will never be the same.

Many people come up to me and ask how we can go month after month preaching the gospel of the Lord Jesus Christ. How is it possible to maintain such a rigid and exhausting schedule? How can a man night after night since Father's Day 1995 stand behind the pulpit with a seemingly one-track mind and preach the same Good News over and over again? Doesn't he grow weary of leading the people in the same prayer he prays each night, "Dear Jesus, speak to my heart. Change my life?" "What makes the evangelist tick?" they ask me.

## QUESTIONS, QUESTIONS

BEFORE I ANSWER, I have to ask them a few other important questions:

What caused the Pastor of Brownsville Assembly of God, John Kilpatrick, to rise up for over two years, take hold of the horns of the altar, grab them firmly, and scream out, "Dear God, send revival to our church. Revive us, oh God!" And then, when his prayer was answered and revival fell, what was the force that drove him to come night after night, month after month to minister to literally hundreds of thousands of souls who poured through the doors at the Brownsville revival meetings while still pastoring his own flock?

What caused the congregation of Brownsville Assembly of God to turn over their elegant but practical sanctuary to total strangers for more than two years? (Strangers who unknowingly placed themselves firmly in a pew that had been marked by a Brownsville family member for years.) What caused these members to smile, find another seat in the balcony or in an overflow room just to make sure the visitor was comfortable (without ever saying, "Hey, they're sitting in my pew!")? What caused the members to be excited and thrilled over this mass of humanity flooding their church? (Can anyone imagine the amount of electricity, water, and even something so menial as toilet paper used during a revival that went on for three years!)

What has motivated a man like Dr. Michael Brown, a scholar's scholar who has traveled extensively unveiling the deep teachings of God, a man who has written numerous bestselling books on revival, a man fluent in Hebrew and Greek, to cancel his life and come to revival night after night to work these altars, pray for the sick, and call down rain from heaven on dry and thirsty Christians? What has caused Dr. Brown, (a man who debates rabbis—and wins!—on the fact that Jesus is the Jewish Messiah) to say to me, "Steve, this is what I've been praying for all my life"? Doesn't he ever grow tired of believing God for total deliverance for those bound and shackled with life-controlling problems who attend our services? What would cause him to move his family here and then serve as president of the new Brownsville Revival School of Ministry (which he helped found), where he pours his life and knowledge into hundreds of hungry students? When he could be at any university in the world, why would Dr. Michael Brown be in Pensacola, of all places?

What has caused another Messianic Jew, Dick Rueben, to move to Pensacola, almost eliminating outside engagements, to be actively involved in this wonderful move of God? Hardly a week goes by where you won't find this ex-biker/turned evangelist, with a shofar (a ram's horn, trumpet) at his lips, piercing the darkness, invoking a shout of victory from the crowd.

What has caused Carey Robertson, a seasoned pastor who moved to Pensacola with intentions of retiring, to find himself laboring night after night in this mighty harvest field?

What is the source of energy that brought Lindell Cooley, Brownsville's minister of music, into Brownsville Assembly to sing for hours, many times to the point of endangering his own precious vocal chords, in order to lead thousands of people—most of whom he will never know—into the presence of God? What has kept him committed to the relentless pace of these revival meetings, when he could have been enjoying a stellar career in the Christian music industry?

What is the motivating factor behind youth pastor, Richard Crisco, who burns himself up for God night after night caring for hundreds of young people, laboring over them with tears? Why would he work so diligently in the day-in, day-out rigors of youth ministry and still make time to help organize dozens of Christian rallies in local public schools and find housing for youth groups from around the country who want to attend the revival? What is it that motivated him to start a True Love Waits (absti-

4

nence from sex before marriage) campaign in the local schools for teens?

Why would the music ministry team of Brownsville Assembly of God come night after night into the sanctuary, often weary from a full day outside, just to face a full night inside? I've watched them juggle family, children, and work to spend the remainder of their energy leading thousands into the presence of God. What has moved them to serve God with their musical gifts and talents? And the choir, faithfully ministering in three of the five revival services per week—what keeps them going?

I could go on and on about the prayer team who, often weary from a hard day's work, slops through the muck of a muddy makeshift parking lot, moves quickly into the prayer room, meets together before the service with other warriors to bind Satan from their lives and the lives of those attending the revival services. They pray together for heaven to come down, and then they march out into the sanctuary like soldiers to pray for and bless thousands of people they don't even know and may never see again, at least on the face of this earth.

What is it that motivates Lyla Terhune and the intercessors who spend time in the back prayer room during the services, agonizing over the souls of the lost? They can be found weeping and wailing, often travailing as a woman giving birth, not for themselves but for the salvation of others. What causes them not to flinch at the thought of waging heated spiritual warfare during this revival?

What brings men like Elmer Melton, Bill Bush, Charles Bailey, R. L. Berry, and the volunteer police force to these meetings? Why do our special security people volunteer to watch over the crowd inside and outside the church each night? Why do scores of men slip on their blue blazers, clip on their usher tags, and come to Brownsville to serve night after night, finding seats for tired visitors, notifying those whose car lights were left on, and loving the various drug addicts and alcoholics who wander in each night? Most of these faithful men daily work blue-collar jobs, yet still come each night to volunteer.

I could go on and on about men like Steve Whitehead (head of Brownsville media ministries), the sound crew, the musicians, all of whom come faithfully each night with the same tenacity to see God move. And what about Van Lane, the children's pastor, who is at the revival every night, counseling young kids who have come to know Jesus as their Savior?

What motivates Christians like those I've mentioned to come into this place with unsaved friends and colleagues, believing in their hearts that God will perform a miracle? What moves Christian students of local high schools to spend hours seeking God and praying for revival on their campuses? Why do we find them night after night in the revival services gripping the hand of an unsaved friend?

What, I have to ask, is going on here?

## THE HEART OF THE ANSWER

WHAT IS IT that motivates us? I believe the answer is in the Bible, the Word of God. We are experiencing firsthand what the apostle Paul experienced two thousand years ago. He had a deep-rooted motivation to do the ministry God had given him, and we have the same deep motivation to do what we are doing. What is that motivates us? Paul identifies it clearly in 1 Corinthians 9:16: "For though I preach the gospel, I have nothing to glory of: for necessity is laid upon me; yea, woe is unto me, if I preach not the gospel!"

In other words, Paul was saying to the Corinthians that

it would be nothing short of tragedy if he did not do what God required of him. "Oh, the horror of it!" Paul proclaimed. In fact, he believed it would be a great calamity if he did *not* preach the glad tidings of the gospel!

Three things passionately motivated Paul to make such a bold declaration concerning his vocation. They are the same three things which move the people of Brownsville and me to respond to God's leading in this incredible revival:

1. Jesus Christ had radically changed his life;
2. Jesus Christ had compelled him to preach the gospel—and woe unto him if he disobeyed.
3. He could not get out of his mind those who had been blinded by the god of this world and did not know the Lord Jesus Christ.

## A PERSONAL THING

BEFORE GOING into these three aspects of Paul's ministry, let's look first at his incredible conversion story:

> And Saul, yet breathing out threatenings and slaughter against the disciples of the Lord, went unto the high priest, and desired of him letters to Damascus to the synagogues, that if he found any of this way, whether they were men or women, he might bring them bound unto Jerusalem. And as he journeyed, he came near Damascus: and suddenly there shined round about him a light from heaven: And he fell to the earth, and heard a voice saying unto him, Saul, Saul, why persecutest thou me?
> And he said, Who art thou, Lord? And the Lord said, I am Jesus whom thou persecutest: it is hard for

thee to kick against the pricks. And he trembling and astonished said, Lord, what wilt thou have me to do? And the Lord said unto him, Arise, and go into the city, and it shall be told thee what thou must do.

And the men which journeyed with him stood speechless, hearing a voice, but seeing no man. And Saul arose from the earth; and when his eyes were opened, he saw no man: but they led him by the hand and brought him into Damascus. And he was three days without sight, and neither did eat nor drink . . . And Ananias went his way, and entered into the house; and putting his hands on him said, Brother Saul, the Lord, even Jesus, that appeared unto thee in the way as thou camest, hath sent me, that thou might receive thy sight, and be filled with the Holy Ghost. And immediately there fell from his eyes as it had been scales: and he received sight forthwith, and arose, and was baptized.

—ACTS 9:1–9, 17–18

This remarkable account suggests that Paul's ministry would be like his conversion: radical. He was saved from a wretched life of self-righteousness and violent acts against Christians; only the gracious God of the universe could see enough in Paul to allow him to become one of the church's most extraordinary missionaries.

Because Paul was radically saved, his mission was never a matter of, "Hmm. I wonder if I should talk about my relationship with Jesus to other people?" God Almighty had visited him and totally changed his life. Paul had been delivered from the kingdom of darkness and translated into the kingdom of light; he went from believing lies to trusting in truth, and so he could not keep quiet about

Jesus. He had not only had a name change from Saul to Paul, but he had gone from *persecuting* the followers of the teachings of Jesus Christ to *promoting* His teachings. In a nutshell, Jesus Christ had powerfully and wonderfully changed his life and "Woe—*what a calamity*—if he did not talk about it!"

The same is true for me and for the people at Brownsville Assembly of God!

A similar, more contemporary version might be the following: The Publishing Sweepstakes has just pulled up in your driveway. You've been broke for some time, trying to make ends meet, never able to get ahead, living under a mountain of bills, sinking in the quicksand of mortgage payments, hospital bills, car payments, and clothes for the kids. Your sixteen-year-old daughter has just asked you for a new pair of blue jeans. You sigh in frustration. Then the doorbell rings.

"Are you so and so?" the sweepstakes representatives ask you. "That's me," you respond. "What can I do for you?"

"It's not what *you* can do for *us* but what *we* have for *you,*" they say. Cameras are rolling and they announce that you are this year's grand prize winner of 1.2 million dollars!

I doubt if you would respond by smugly saying, "Wow, that's great! But could you excuse me, please? I'm watching my favorite bass-fishing program on television. They're demonstrating a new 'super vibrating, fluorescent, guaranteed-to-catch-'em-or-your-money-back' lure for largemouth bass. Hey, gotta go. Thanks for the check."

Sorry, friend, I don't think so. You would go wild, scream, shout, do a back flip, anything but go inside and watch some ridiculous television program. After the impact of winning the check hits you, you would burn up the local phone lines, calling friends and family with your good news. You would probably even call your enemies!

Any unexpected, life-changing gift is exciting. But when a man is saved from the debt of sin and despair through the good news of God's love, it's worth far more than millions of dollars! No wonder Paul said it would be a horror for him *not* to preach of the One who brought him out of darkness.

I can relate. I, too, have been delivered from a life of darkness, delivered from a drug addiction that for years had kept me from living the kind of life God called me to. Preaching the gospel is now what I must do.

Jesus Christ changed Paul's life. Jesus Christ changed my life too. Jesus Christ has changed the lives of countless thousands at Brownsville Assembly of God and in our revival. We cannot stop talking about it! Just like Peter and John in Acts 4:20, "We cannot but speak the things which we have seen and heard."

Paul's fervor, like ours, to preach the gospel was a result of the white-hot fire of the Holy Ghost coming in and burning up every piece of trash that was sitting around his spiritual house. The Lord had annihilated in him every desire for human recognition and fame; he preached Christ and Christ crucified because he had personally experienced the transforming power of the Lord.

We are all like Jeremiah, who wrote in 20:9: "But his [God's] word was in mine heart as a burning fire shut up in my bones." Like Jeremiah, Paul could no longer hold it in; the holy fire burned in his soul.

And so we have gone from being a slave of Satan and sin to being a bondservant of the Lord Jesus Christ. We cannot *not* serve him. Woe unto us if we do not share this life-changing news! It would be a great calamity to us not to do so. It is a personal thing!

## COMPELLED TO PREACH

JESUS CHRIST had compelled Paul to preach the gospel, and woe unto him if he disobeyed. It is the same for us in revival. From the moment of his conversion, Paul was marked. Acts 9:15 confirms this: "For he is a chosen vessel unto me, to bear my name before the Gentiles, and kings, and the children of Israel." In other words, Paul was under obligation to the Lord.

In 1849, the godly scholar Noah Webster defined *obligation* in *The American Dictionary of the English Language* as "the binding power of a vow or oath; that which constitutes legal or moral duty, and which renders a person liable to coercion and punishment for neglecting. The laws and commands of God impose on us an obligation to love Him supremely and our neighbor as ourselves."[1] Webster's original definition teaches us that an obligation is a serious matter that, if neglected, has equally serious consequences or punishment.

Friend, the bottom line is that God had entrusted Paul with the gospel. What was he going to do? Bury it in the sand and go about his merry (or his un-merry) way? He had a "binding oath," a "moral duty" to love God supremely and his neighbor as himself. For him, that meant preaching the gospel. Paul's every act and word were spent communicating the truth that had so radically changed his life.

For those of us whose lives have also been changed by the truth, we can do no less.

## REACHING THE LOST

WE HAVE learned that Paul had been drastically changed by the gospel; therefore he was obligated to share it. He was commanded of the Lord to do so, and it would have been a tragedy or calamity not to. Yet, the third and final reason for his "Woe unto me" statement was his love for the unknowing multitudes, those who did not yet know the love of Christ.

The love of Christ controlled Paul, as he said in 2 Corinthians 5:14, "The love of Christ constrains" or controls him. Paul, like us, had an unquenchable zeal to see the lost saved, to see the spiritually blind open their eyes, to see the bound delivered, and to see those without hope, those brokenhearted, healed and rejoicing in the new life found only in Christ.

The lost of Paul's day were the same as the lost of today. The more I read history and the Word of God, the more I am struck with the similarities of lost people without God (and that includes all of us). People have always pursued other gains, worshiped other idols, turned their backs on their Maker, and "changed the truth of God into a lie and worshiped and served the creature more than the Creator, who is blessed for ever" (Rom. 1:25). Paul desperately wanted them to be set free.

This same burden for the lost is at the heart of the Brownsville revival. We are like Paul, crying "woe unto us" if we do not give everyone an opportunity to know the Lord. We want everyone who comes to the services to experience the joy of waking up the next morning at peace with themselves and God. We want everyone to experience the blessedness of not having to fret about the future. We want everyone to experience the sparkling-clean feeling of being washed in the blood of the Lamb.

The Bible says, "Whosoever shall call upon the name of the Lord shall be saved" (Rom. 10:13). That means everyone can experience the saving grace of Christ. We want everyone to stop living in defeat and experience vic-

torious living. We want everyone to learn how to lean on
the promises of God, to be delivered from life-controlling
problems and addictions, to move on from a past that is
forgiven and forgotten to a heavenly hope.

Woe unto us, to those of us in Pensacola, Florida, to
Christians everywhere, if we do not preach the gospel of
the Lord Jesus Christ. Leonard Ravenhill gave me the following poem by Charles Wesley that best sums this up.
(He suggested I paste it in the back of my Bible and read it
each time I got ready to preach):

> Shall I, in fear of mortal man,
>     The Spirit's course in me restrain?
> Or, undismayed, in deed and word
>     Be a true witness to my Lord?
> Awed by a mortal's frown, shall I
>     Conceal the Word of God most high?
> How then before Thee shall I dare
>     To stand, or how Thine anger bare?
> What then is whose scorn I dread,
>     Whose wrath or hate makes me afraid?
> A man? an heir of death, a slave
>     To sin? a bubble on the wave!
> Yet let men rage, since Thou wilt spread
>     Thy shadowing wings about my head;
> Since in all pain Thy tender love
>     Will still my sure refreshment prove.
> Give me Thy strength, O God of power;
>     Then let winds blow or tempests roar;
> Thy faithful witness will be;
>     'Tis fixed; I can do all through Thee.

"Shall I conceal the Word of God most high?" No! I
firmly believe we would experience a great calamity if we

did not do what God has gloriously called us to. We simply cannot contain ourselves; Christ has changed us, and His love compels us each day. Oh, that each reader of this book might know the same compelling love!

That is why all these things are happening at Brownsville Assembly of God. It is why drug addicts and prostitutes, businessmen and teachers alike are getting saved; why marriages and families are being brought back together in powerful ways; why pastors, leaders, and seekers from all over the world are coming to Pensacola for a fresh touch from God; why spiritually hungry people of all economic and ethnic backgrounds are experiencing a new sense of repentance and renewal.

Revival has come.

The Holy Spirit of the Living God is moving in our lives like never before. But for me, it has not always been like this. I am an unlikely evangelist who considers himself privileged to be preaching at this revival. Twenty-five years ago, though, many would not have believed it would happen. I was as lost as lost could be.

One of the reasons the message of Christ is preached with such urgency and clarity is because, as the evangelist, I will never forget what He's delivered me from. Each night when I gaze out at the sea of faces, my heart returns to the days without Christ, without hope. I know, in every service, hundreds will be listening who need to hear about His love and forgiveness. Yes, I remember what it was like to be lost.

*Chapter Two*

# Stone-Cold Heart

*A new heart also will I give you, and a new spirit will I put within you: and I will take away the stony heart out of your flesh, and I will give you an heart of flesh.*
—EZEKIEL 36:26

THE DARKNESS WAS DEAFENING. In my drug-crazed, deathly condition came a voice inside my head, "This is it, Steve."

*Am I awake or asleep?* I wondered. *Am I alive or dead? Is this real, or am I hallucinating?*

Slowly, my body began to go into convulsions. *Yes, this must be real! I'm going to die.* I thought. *Just let it happen like everything else in your life. Let death come.*

The thought of dying, of suicide, had filled my mind for months. Thinking of getting off the painful treadmill of my life—jail, alcohol, confusion, hatred, loneliness, hurt, and misery—brought the slightest hope and comfort as I lay in the dark bedroom I had grown up in. The drugs I had taken for years no longer offered any high. Hope, love, or thinking of others had long left me. Yes, death surely would be a relief.

*But it's not happening like I planned,* I thought. *It's supposed to be a peaceful release. What is this horrible cloud of darkness and pain?*

My legs and arms, out of control, began shaking wildly. I couldn't get up, and I couldn't relax. Instead of coming peacefully, death was choking me, saying, "Just give in, just give in."

Though my body convulsed in violent agony—one part wanting to die, another wanting to live—my fear somehow was now motivating me to live. Weakly but intently, I began to fight.

I yelled to my mother, the only one who still cared about this pitiful shell of a person. I could barely tell she was there; my eyes couldn't focus clearly, and I was still convulsing. My body was in violent withdrawal from all the drugs I had dumped into it throughout my twenty-one years of living.

"Son, son!" she cried with fear. "What's wrong? You're pouring sweat and shaking!" Only as her hands touched mine did I realize my heart was beating wildly. Momentarily, her touch brought some relief to the turbulence in my mind. Tears as I had never known them welled up and streamed down my face.

My mother covered me with a blanket and stroked my forehead. I tried desperately to focus to see her.

"What is happening to me, Mama? I'm dying! I'm dying!" I cried again and again. "Help me, Mama, help me! Stop the pain. Somebody, stop the pain!"

But neither of us knew how to stop it. Every piece of

furniture, every picture, every article in the room felt as if it were covered with death. The walls swelled in and out. It was a nightmare of horror—only I was awake to experience it firsthand. And all the time, the voice of evil persisted to whisper its desperate deception: "Give in, give in. There is no way out. Your life is over, Steve. There is no more. It's time to end it. Let me help you."

## EVIL'S PERSISTENCE

IT WAS THE SAME VOICE that over the years I had come to identify as my own. Now in my dying state, however, I finally recognized the voice for what it was: *evil.* Still, in my body's violent reaction to drug withdrawal I could find no relief, no comfort. My mother couldn't help me, no one could, and I definitely could not bear to have my brother or sisters see me in such a helpless condition.

The pain and agony continued for days—days that were no less painful than the nights. In fact, those nights were the longest I have ever had before or since. My dear mother sat by me hour after hour, but death's shadow never left me.

In my delirium, my mind played games with me. My thoughts took me back to my childhood and youth. . . . I was at the cookie jar. Though my mother had told me not to eat any cookies before supper, my six-year-old senses told me I simply had to taste her freshly baked cookies. I openly disobeyed, and was not caught. Yes, my conscience let me know I had done wrong; I was guilty, I had given in to my selfish voice, and now I did not like this guilty feeling. I wished for it to go away, but it didn't.

The problems and guilt grew within me. "Stevie, why are you always bothering your sister?" "For the last time, Stevie, get in bed and stay there." "If you do that one more time, I'm going to have your father punish you. . . . " The young boy with his toys and wonderful family was changing. It wasn't intentional. Misbehaving was just becoming natural.

The voice of selfish evil that had gotten me the cookies from the cookie jar was now convincing me that he was my friend, the one to lead and guide me. My parents constantly tried to correct me. But with four children they did more threatening than spanking, more warning than disciplining. Besides, I was becoming very adept at disobeying. I rarely got caught. More and more, I appeared to be one kind of child to my parents, another to my brother and sisters, and still another to my friends and classmates.

The voice was consistently there, even at the store after school. One time I saw a shiny, black toy cap pistol on the rack. Would Mom buy it for me? She'd probably say, "Stevie, you need to save for it with your allowance." But that would take weeks and I wanted it *now!* I looked around the store aisle. No one was there. My hands began to sweat, I wanted that pistol so badly. And the evil voice urged me, "Go ahead, take it. They have plenty."

Inside, another voice was also trying to speak. "Steve, you know that's wrong. That is stealing, and you are going to get into big trouble."

The evil voice won out. With great paranoia, I eased the cap pistol off the rack and under my shirt. When I slipped out of the store undetected, I told myself, "You did it! You beat the system again. It will be easier next time."

And it was easier the next time . . . and the next time . . . and the next. Being able to succeed at lying and stealing without getting caught seemed to magnify my desire to do more wrong. Shoplifting, burglary, stealing from purses and wallets, cursing, lying, and cheating had all became part of my young personality.

By age twelve, I had put myself in dozens of compromising situations and faced fears that many people never experience in a lifetime. I was caught in evil's web of greed, sin, and selfishness. My life was under someone's control—yet, it wasn't *me* who was controlling it.

By my teenage years, I did not have toy guns; I had real ones, along with knives. I had all the candy and the cigarettes, all the clothes I wanted, all the right accessories to impress my friends. Still, deep down I was not happy. My classmates, even some of the "straights," seemed happy, yet they did not have half the possessions that I had. So what was the problem?

At that point in my life, I certainly never considered the problem to be who I was listening to and following. My course was set. It was full-speed ahead and I wasn't sure things could ever be changed.

## A HEART OF STONE

"STEVE," MOM CALLED. "Turn that noise down! It's so loud I can't hear myself think!"

On the radio, "I Can't Get No Satisfaction" was blasting, my favorite song by the Rolling Stones. It said it all for my generation. Materially, we had everything. But there was still something missing, and we had to get out and search for it, each in our own way. The decade of the 1960s was the age of discovery—of throwing off the old and trying on the new, of searching for new values, new freedoms, anything that would satisfy us in the moment. As a teenager, I was much too young to understand or evaluate the politics, ethics, or consequences of it all. But I was old enough to taste and experiment.

That is when I decided I would discover what it would feel like to get high, to drink, and to get drunk. I wanted to smoke pot and get stoned. I wanted to know what it was like to flip out on an LSD trip. So many of the older kids were talking about the thrill of doing it. Even some of my classmates bragged that they had tried these new drugs. I didn't know if they were just lying to "be popular" the way I did, or whether they had really done them.

The evil voice echoed inside me, "It's a whole new world. *Everybody* is doing drugs! They won't hurt you. You can control them!" My parents and teachers had clearly warned me against drug and alcohol abuse. But between my rebellious peers and the voice of my "guide," I was hooked before I ever lifted a beer bottle or smoked my first joint. Attending the many large rock festivals in our area, seeing thousands of young people such as myself gathered together and getting high, made it seem all right.

At home, my brother and sisters acted so good. Then there was me. Why was I the rebel, the black sheep? The questions plagued me. Finally, I concluded that I was destined to be bad and that I would never "fit in" with my family. What I did not know then, of course, was the truth: all of us are born in sin and selfishness, even if we hide it from others.

My guilt separated me from receiving any of the love my family still had for me. I detested being at home because it magnified my guilt. So I lived and yearned for parties and running with the crowd that was hustling trouble.

At age thirteen, I was smoking cigarettes, drinking, smoking marijuana, and even tripping out on pills. These drugs changed my whole way of thinking. I found that the bottle, joint, or pill could temporarily eradicate the guilt, eliminate the confusion, and deliver me from my feelings of isolation. It did not matter to me that the feelings induced by these drugs were all lies. I didn't care, as long as I could buy more drugs and get high again.

The next year I joined a rock music group, the first of many over the next few years. Music was the principal medium of my new lifestyle. We sang songs that spoke of freedom, love, getting high—songs that promised escape. Being in a rock-and-roll band opened all kinds of new doors for my rebellious lifestyle. We played at high-school dances, pool parties, clubs, and private jams where there was always an abundance of drugs and alcohol. I was a young performer, and the attention was fantastic. There was always something to do, some place to go, something new to try. It was a season for the pleasures of sin.

Would the party end? Would the ride stop? I hoped not. In the uncertain times of the late sixties and early seventies, everyone lived just for the day. By sixteen, I had experimented with every kind of drug sold on the street. School was a fog to me—total boredom, a waste of time. I no longer kept up with my classmates (except those in the drug culture) because none of their world had any appeal. Studies had long since lost my interest. Teachers passed me to get me out of their classes, so that amazingly, I stayed in school, playing the silly games.

I was now taking more and more drugs to get high. But our community police were cracking down; drugs were harder to find and becoming more expensive. Some of my friends began quitting school, unable to concentrate on their studies. Many ended up in jail.

## DEEPER DESPAIR

THEN CAME THE GREATEST tragedy of my teenage years. It happened at the beginning of school one brisk spring morning. I was sitting in my homeroom when my name was paged over the school intercom. "Stephen Hill, please report to the principal's office immediately."

What had I done now? Had the police discovered I was selling drugs and come to arrest me? A hundred thoughts of guilt and fear filled my mind as I made the slow, familiar trek to the principal's office.

As the secretary showed me into the office, I realized this time was different. The principal had a whole different look today. Something tragic must have happened! Placing his hands on my shoulders and looking me in the eyes, the principal said softly, "Steve, your dad has died. It was a heart attack last night in his sleep. Your mother thought he was just sleeping, but when she tried to wake him this morning, he was gone. I'm so sorry about this. Your neighbor is coming to pick you up."

He just kept looking at me, with his hands still on my shoulder. I guess he assumed I would cry. But I didn't. *I couldn't.* I had become so detached and hardened, I couldn't think or feel anything. Someone I had known and loved was gone, someone important in my life, but what did it matter?

Being at home in the days after my dad's death was strange. All sorts of people came over to console, comfort, and share our silence with us. The voice of conscience pricked my heart for the first time in many months: "You should be helping your mom in her grief. You're old enough, and you should be helping your brother and sisters." But everything that I thought to say or do seemed so shallow, so immature. I hadn't realized that besides my emotional detachment from my family, three years of drug abuse had stopped my psychological development. Consequently, I was really shallow and immature.

The solution? To get away from these people who were so honestly and openly dealing with their hurt and grief. I went to my room, shut the door, and closed myself off from reality.

Soon that friendly, evil voice was back. "Don't worry, Steve. You really didn't know your dad all that well. Besides, you're living your own life now. You don't have to cry just because somebody wants you to. In reality, nothing has changed for you."

The voice went on: "What you need right now are some pills to get you through this time. Don't worry about the feelings of your family. They will be okay. You're different. You need some help to get you through."

The right phone call, out the back door, and soon I was hooked up. The painful reality of my dad's death became just a fog. I stayed stoned until after the funeral, even as I stood with my flesh-and-blood family while they lowered my father's body into the grave. They were remembering the good times, clutching one another closely to fill the void. I stood there empty, emotionless, distant. When our family needed one another most, I couldn't give myself. I was far away. My heart was sealed . . . cold . . . a heart of stone. How ironic that the very drug world I had entered to *enhance* my feelings had now sealed me away so that I was emotionally paralyzed.

I had chosen my lot.

## GOING NOWHERE

THROUGH THE YEARS my father had represented at least a semblance of God's authority that bound me to certain rules at home. Now, he was gone, and my mom was trying desperately to get her own life back together while caring for her children. It was impossible for her to carry out the enforcement of any regulations. That meant I was free to do whatever I wanted, whenever I wanted. Unwittingly, she was enabling my drug abuse by allowing me to stay in her home with no rules or responsibilities.

Life became more of a nightmare, full of ups and downs. One day I'd have the desire to excel and make something of myself; the next day I'd be dragged down, totally wasted, overdosed on drugs. I was constantly led down the school corridors to the principal's office. Expelled from school again!

My life was going nowhere. My acquaintances (you couldn't call them friends, because in reality we cared for drugs and highs more than for each other) were sinking lower into death. Many of them had begun using the needle to inject narcotics. Just looking at them, I could see the destruction process, and it should have frightened me far away. But it didn't. I simply had no other place to go.

Knowing that using the needle would mean physical addiction, and that addiction meant sickness, pain, and probably death, I wondered why anyone would do it. Still, it meant getting "higher," "freer"—and I was desperate for some new high, some new meaning, anything. In the end, the voice of self said, "Go ahead. Go along with the others. Just be careful. *You* can control it. *You* won't get addicted."

As I melted the morphine into the spoon and drew it into the needle, the last hint of my conscience warned, "This will mean destruction to you." But it was too late. The needle pressed against my skin. No one else was making me do it. The evil voice had become me. I said, "Go ahead. Push that needle in." And I did.

The blood from the puncture wound dripped off my arm, and my mind made its foggy, hazy way into oblivion. Each time my last thoughts would be, *Steve, you are now a full-fledged drug addict. You have become nothing . . . nothing . . . nothing.* Then darkness came, gross darkness and oblivion, my only peace. There was no such thing as controlling my addiction; I lived for the next fix.

More narcotics meant more money, which meant more crime, more rip-offs. We became a desperate band of wolves, stealing, devouring anything that stood in our way. Even our own families weren't safe from our consuming need for money to do drugs. The cycle of drugs-crime-jail, drugs-crime-jail repeated over and over and could only be stopped by death itself.

First, there was Manny. He had come up short once too often in paying our supplier for his heroin. We found Manny one morning with multiple stab wounds in his heart. It was meant to be a lesson to us, but we never were good learners.

Frankie was next. He must have forgotten how much heroin he had put in that last injection. Lying in his girl-friend's arms, he just quit breathing and was gone forever.

Toby self-destructed in a drunken stupor in his car, wrapped around a telephone pole. Sammy drove across the wrong side of a highway and met death on the broad side of a truck.

For my good friend, Bobbie, it had all become too much. We were arrested together, but Bobbie never came out on his feet. He hung himself in jail.

Surely, I was on the death list, too, somewhere. Where, when, how would it end? I didn't want to think about it. I had to get away, to run, to hide from death. But where?

Without any direction, I hitchhiked around the country. Wherever I could find shelter, I would stop: in caves, under bridges, in the desert, in street missions. My companions were the refuse of life. Stealing was all we knew, and there was no honor code among us. We'd steal from one another as easily as from a store, home, or even a church.

And when all else failed, we would end up at the Red Cross office. There was always a line of drug addicts and alcoholics at the clinic to sell blood and get money for a habit. The nurses hid their eyes from ours as we sold ourselves for the next high.

On that bleak road to oblivion, we met every kind of religious guru and philosopher you can imagine. In our deception and vanity, we would argue endlessly about the proper course of life. All the time, we were sitting in the deepest possible pit of muck and darkness. It must have been comical, I'm sure, for people to hear our crazy philosophical dissertations and religious incantations that made no sense to anyone but ourselves.

## A Flame of Hope

SOMEONE ONCE TOLD ME how the wisest man who ever lived, King Solomon, had warned that every person has a direction he feels is right. He honestly believes his illusion. The problem, according to Solomon, was that this illusion will one day end. In the final analysis, many people will find that their way in life was incorrect, and the result will be eternal death.

Was there a chance I could discover the folly of my life before it was too late?

Would I listen to anyone? No. Would I pay attention to the reality that so many friends had died? No. What hope was left? Like a straw floating in the wind, I drifted aimlessly, running from certain death.

One day, a friend and I stumbled into a free concert in a large park in Dallas, Texas. Over five thousand people were there enjoying the contemporary, positive music. But what appealed to us most were the free sandwiches being handed out. Everything was cool until the musicians began to share their message. The guitarist talked about his life before he met Jesus Christ and compared it to his present life as a Christian.

"I was a loser, nobody," he said. "But Jesus came into my heart and changed my whole life. He has given me His all. Now every day is wonderful, and Jesus has a plan for your life too. He loves each and every one of you. He wants to forgive you and create in you a clean heart."

To me, this was just another religious guru, trying to convert me to his way of thinking. But to my friend, the guitarist was proclaiming truth. He said, "Steve, I think I'm going up there to talk with that man about Jesus. I want to be a Christian."

I suddenly got angry. "You fool," I shouted at him. "If you believe this garbage about Jesus Christ and ask for forgiveness, your whole life will be governed by rules and that junk. You won't be able to drink, smoke, do drugs, have sex, curse, or anything else. Besides, all they want is your money."

The venom with which I lashed out surprised me. Why was I so adamant to protect this friend from Christianity? What was it to me if he wanted to change and give up this maddening life? What was it about this Christianity that upset me? Surely, I had tried just about everything a human being could do in this world. Why was I afraid of this Jesus? Why was I fighting Him?

I pulled my friend in the other direction, and we left the park together. I thought, *That was a close call. No religion is going to control my life with its lies.* Instead, we got high. Again.

We also ended up in jail. Again. It was becoming my second home. Now, the dry heaving of the drunk in the next bunk was getting on my nerves. The pain and discomfort in my mind and body from drug dependency made any hope of sleep impossible. But what pressed my mind most at the moment was the fear of having to fight any or all of the "animals" in this cell-block who might decide to choose me as their next target to rape. My long, dirty blond hair and light complexion made me a likely target. Whenever I was incarcerated by myself without a friend, I always made it a point to befriend some "heavy" by sharing my cigarettes, talking trash, telling about my crimes, and planning some new score, even if we were just blowing smoke.

Surviving in the pit of human refuse had become my lifestyle. No longer did I even try to lie to get the judge to let me off from punishment for my crimes. This was partly because I usually didn't remember what I had done under the influence of narcotics to end up in jail. Yet somehow, the judges did not want to waste the taxpayers' money on me and usually gave me a short jail sentence or probation.

When I'd get out, it would be just long enough to commit more crimes for money enough to get drunk or high before being locked up. Again. More and more, my thoughts turned to Bobbie, who had hung himself in jail. Maybe that *was* the only way out. Here I was; I had not yet celebrated my twenty-first birthday, and I felt like my life was over.

My mind and body were burned out. Suicide became more and more appealing. Thoughts of death . . . the ultimate escape . . . filled my mind.

## DEATH DEFEATED

THAT IS WHEN I FOUND myself back in my mother's home. On that dramatic Saturday morning of October 25, 1975, the death angel visited me for the last time. During the next three days, convulsions racked my body while the dark cloud of death hovered over my room, my mind, and my life.

Day and night, my mother sat beside me. But only a

Power greater than both of us enabled me to live through those hellish days and nights. Sometime during this nightmare, two life-changing revelations came to me.

The first was something I'd known as a child, but had long since forgotten: that the evil voice that led and ruled me was not me. It had possessed and controlled me, but it was not me. The second, I realized for the first time, was that this evil voice and power was the Destroyer. His intention all along was not to help me, but to destroy me.

Now I no longer wanted that power in me. I wanted to be free from its destruction. But how? Its force held me in bondage. All I could do was lie there and try to resist, knowing that my strength and resistance were failing fast.

On Tuesday morning, October 28, as I lay in my helpless condition, I heard a knock on the door. I didn't want to see anyone, but I needed help desperately. Outside my room, I heard my mother talking with a young vicar from St. Mark's Lutheran Church, Rev. Hugh Mozingo, who had recently moved into our town and tried to reach out to me. I found out later that Mom had called the church stating that there was an emergency at home—she needed a pastor to come over quickly.

My mom let him into my room. He began, "I know that you didn't want anything to do with me before, Steve. But I've come because you are hurting. I can't help you, but I know somebody who can. His name is Jesus, and He's here with us. He's my best friend, Steve, and He wants to help you."

Tears that had been bottled up during fifteen years of rebellion, hurt, and bitterness suddenly began to flow down my cheeks. The evil presence was still around me. My body was still racked with convulsions. My mind was still clouded with confusion. But here was someone offering hope.

Like always, I was not about to play religious games. The vicar would have to overcome my doubts and unbelief. I protested. "I haven't ever believed in Jesus. I have never prayed to a god in my life. How do I know this Jesus is alive?"

"Steve, you are going to have to trust me in this," he said. "Jesus is here in this room, and He'll touch your life if you'll just cry out to Him. You don't need to say a fancy prayer. God knows your heart. Just cry out the name, *Jesus! Jesus!*"

The sound of that name again and again seemed to bring hope from nowhere. The confusion and fear faded slowly as I looked to the ceiling and began to utter, *"Jesus, Jesus, Jesus, Jesus!"*

A peace, a warmth such as I never felt before, flooded my body. This power rushed in like a river and took command of everything. I kept crying out His name, louder and louder: *"Jesus! Jesus! Jesus!"* The more I said it, the greater was my deliverance. The convulsions stopped. The evil presence vanished. The pulsating walls in my room stood still!

Almost immediately, I felt the room fill with another Presence; this one beautiful and divine. My visitor friend didn't need to tell me what had happened. It was crystal-clear; I had just received the gift of new life in Jesus Christ. He had set me free! For so many years, I had lived in total darkness and bondage to sin. My guilt and sins had covered me like a heavy blanket. But I discovered nothing is too great for our Lord Jesus Christ. The testimony of God's Word declared, "Though your sins be as scarlet, they shall be as white as snow; though they be red like crimson, they shall be as wool," (Isa. 1:18). Now, those words were *my* testimony too.

The Destroyer had held me in his total control. But his

chains were lies. In truth, there *is* hope. Life *is* worth living. I could be changed; I could be healed. And, as the light of God's love shone into my dark room that morning, all these truths burst upon my heart in total deliverance. As Jesus said, "Ye shall know the truth and the truth shall make you free . . . I am the way, the truth, and the life: no man cometh unto the Father, but by me" (John 8:32, 14:6).

On that Tuesday morning, Jesus Christ performed a great miracle: He transformed my heart. I was clean, forgiven, alive again! The truth had set me free!

And I had to tell everyone I knew.

# Chapter Three

# The Light of Life

*The people which sat in darkness saw great light; and to them which sat in the region and shadow of death light is sprung up.*

—MATTHEW 4:16

**M**Y MOM TESTIFIES everywhere that her son was transformed before her eyes. "His face was so hard and cold, but immediately after his experience with Jesus, Steve had the countenance of an innocent child. He looked so happy and free."

There was no doubt: God had delivered me from the domain of darkness and brought me into the fellowship of His marvelous light. The kind Lutheran vicar who came to my mother's house that day had boldly introduced me to the only One who could save my soul, cleanse my heart, and redirect my steps. I was indeed a new person.

A few minutes after my conversion, I found myself outside the house, soaking up the beauty of God's creation. It was a brisk October day in Northern Alabama. The sun was shining and a cool breeze was blowing. Everything was perfect. I remember looking up at the sky and saying, "It's so blue." I reached down and grabbed a handful of grass, ran the blades through my fingers, and said, "It's so green." Everything was new! It was like experiencing life through the eyes of a child. I had been born again.

About that time, a station wagon pulled up in front of the house. Inside the car was a group of my old drug buddies. The driver jumped out, held up a bag of Colombian marijuana, and shouted out, "Let's go get stoned."

Normally, I would have jumped in the car and been gone for hours or even days. But the first thing that came out of my mouth was, "A few minutes ago, Jesus Christ came into my life. I've never felt this good, I've never been so happy. If I smoke that pot with you, all this will go away. I'm sorry, but I don't wanna smoke dope any more." With a puzzled look on his face, he crumpled the bag, stuffed it into his pocket, jumped back in the car, and sped off. I knew that day that nothing would ever be the same.

I began to tell all the people I knew about my strange and wonderful encounter with Jesus Christ. Many thought I was "tripping" on some new drug; others shook their heads, skeptical that I was just "conning" them again with another story. Time would tell whether or not my conversion was real. It was true, I told them. I had been delivered from drug abuse, set free from its horrible bondage, and I was excited about my new faith.

But like any new believer, I was about to find out that submitting to the Lord Jesus Christ did not mean life would suddenly be easy. This new Christian lifestyle would certainly be challenged by the prince of darkness.

## ENTERING THE BATTLE

ONE DAY NOT LONG AFTER that first time I called on the name of Jesus, I was walking across the parking lot of a local grocery store. It was a cool Alabama day and my heart was peaceful for the first time in years. As I got closer to the building, I glanced down at the black tar. Right in front of my nose lay a brand-new, unopened pack of cigarettes. Not just any pack, either; it was the same favorite brand that I had smoked two to three packs a day of since I was nearly ten years.

I stopped in my tracks. Then I heard that old familiar voice whispering in my ear again, "Isn't this luck? Wouldn't one of these taste great right now? It is all right. Nobody is around to see." I listened, faced with my first temptation since becoming a Christian. There was only one difference, though, between the old Steve and the new Christian Steve with regard to that voice. Now I had the discernment of the Holy Spirit to recognize that voice as the Destroyer. I knew at that moment that I had entered a very different battle.

Reaching down, I picked up the pack of cigarettes, stared at it, and slowly smiled. Without a second thought, I crumpled those cigarettes in my fist and said out loud right there in the parking lot, "Satan, you are not going to defeat me! I am a new creature in Christ. My new nature doesn't *need* these cigarettes. You are defeated!"

As I walked toward the trash can, God's Holy Spirit gently reminded me that the cigarettes could be retrieved there. I was to leave no room for Satan to enter.

So I located the nearest public restroom and flushed the entire pack down the toilet. As I watched the cigarettes disappear, I heard the Lord speak to my heart: "Steve, I will always show you a way out of temptation. But you have to be willing to totally destroy every source of temptation, every evil thing that comes your way. As you destroy even the sources of temptation, your thoughts will be established in Me. Remember this truth, and you will be victorious in life."

I breathed a silent, "Thank You, God," and walked into the grocery store, confident of Christ's presence with me.

I knew God's words to me that day were important to listen to. I soon began to face head-on each of the habits that had controlled my life in the past: drugs, alcohol, cursing, and the like. As I did, either the relationships that had been built around these things were broken because of my new stand for Jesus Christ, or people were won to Christ. Within weeks, I was separated from every drug pusher or user friend. It was as if the word "Jesus" spoken in love and respect made them scatter. As is true in football or basketball, the best defense of faith is a good offense—that is, stepping out and witnessing for His name.

The other old habits of lying, hatred, and lust also fell away as I changed what I read, what I said, what I did, and who I spent my time with. I wanted desperately to live the kind of life that would please the One who had so graciously saved me.

## A SURPRISING FOUNDATION

ONE DAY I READ in 1 Peter 2:2, "As newborn babes, desire the sincere milk of the word, that ye may grow thereby." That meant me! The Holy Bible became my map in life. To me it was a guide to treasures—more treasures, in fact, than I could possibly imagine. On every page I found the most wonderful promises from God.

I also found myself praying daily, "Oh, Lord, I have

missed out on so much. I have wasted so many years, and now I am just like a baby. If You are going to restore me and rebuild me, You will have to guide me every step of the way, because I don't know what to do." I hadn't yet met anyone who could tell me how to grow in Christ, so I depended on God to build my foundation.

And He did. He guided me each step of each new day, but not in the way I expected. Within a few short weeks after my conversion, an event took place that radically changed the course of my life. On a cold Saturday night at 11 P.M., a knock came at my door. I answered and found myself face-to-face with a local narcotics agent. He had in his hand four warrants for my arrest on felony charges. I was handcuffed and led off to jail.

My dear mother watched as her son once again was imprisoned. The question entered both of our minds: *Why? Why now, God?* I had changed. I was a new person. These felony charges for drug sales were from the past. *Why now, God?*

Yet, the Bible says in Romans 8:28, "And we know that all things work together for good to them that love God, to them who are called according to his purpose." It also says in Isaiah 55:8, "My thoughts are not your thoughts, neither are your ways my ways." God was teaching me not to trust in my ways but simply to trust Him.

I spent several months in jail, caged like an animal, before I saw the Lord's purpose. While incarcerated, a minister by the name of Jim Summers came by to visit me on a regular basis. Jim ran a drug rehabilitation program called Outreach Ministries of Alabama (OMA). His kindness and concern for me continually encouraged me during those challenging but foundational months in jail.

## UNDESERVED SENTENCING

THROUGH CONVERSATIONS with the judge and my lawyer, Jim was trying his best to have me probated into his program. Outreach Ministries was affiliated with Teen Challenge, another drug rehabilitation program, and both were dedicated to helping give spiritual direction and discipline to young men and women such as myself. If it worked as Jim was trying to arrange, I would spend three months with Outreach Ministries and nine months at Mid-America Teen Challenge in Cape Girardeau, Missouri, under the direction of Herb Meppelink, undergoing intense, accountable rehabilitation.

My heart pounded and my palms sweated as I stood before the judge the day I was to receive my sentence. There was no doubt to anyone that I deserved to get many years in the penitentiary for the crimes I had committed before I became a Christian. I knew I was in trouble when I stood before this particular judge; he had seen me before. I had been on trial for previous offenses many times. Each time I had failed. The judges had always been lenient, giving me probation. This time I expected, and was prepared, to go to prison. I was already on probation for the sale of drugs. This time a prison sentence seemed certain.

The judge calmly raised his eyes from the bench and sternly looked into mine. As he cleared his throat, my heart beat so fast and so loud I thought everyone in the courtroom could hear it. I trembled as the judge began to read his decision: "Stephen Hill, this is against my better judgment and you'd better understand that. Nonetheless, I am going to sentence you to Outreach Ministries of Alabama under the supervision of Jim Summers. If you do not successfully complete that program, you will spend many years in the penitentiary."

My jaw fell open. I wanted to shout "Hallelujah!" but I remained calm before this merciful but tough judge. I will never forget that moment; I knew without a doubt that the Lord Almighty had made a way out for me!

Being "sentenced" to OMA and Teen Challenge was the best thing that could have happened to me. There, I learned to put feet to my faith. I learned to live out my professions of love and faith in Christ. I was established in the basics of Christian living: I was water-baptized, and filled with the Holy Spirit. I learned how to not just read the Bible but to study it, and I became disciplined in prayer.

I also discovered that outward actions or words do not necessarily dictate where a person is with God. In other words, some guys had all the right religious words and "moves" but inwardly they were still playing games with God. Others had genuinely repented of their sins and had come to God, but had not yet learned godly speech and manners. I realized that it was the condition of the heart that God looked at, that only He could give a person a new heart: "And I shall give them one heart, and shall put a new spirit within them. And I shall take the heart of stone out of their flesh and give them a heart of flesh" (Ezek. 11:19, NAS).

God had given me not only a new heart but also a new mind. My mind had been a sewer . . . filled with garbage, lust, hatred, bitterness, despair, and the like. When Jesus set me free, forgave my sins, and came into my heart, He cleansed me of all the filth in my conscious mind. But there was still a whole sea of subconscious garbage that needed cleansing and renewing.

At first, I let the devil hound me with condemnation every time that old thinking surfaced. Then I learned that I could personally come to Jesus and ask for forgiveness and cleansing—anytime, day or night. In fact, God used those old thoughts for good, because every time they came up, they pointed me to Jesus anew for forgiveness, and made me love Him even more for His free grace through the cross. I learned that giving myself, my heart, to Him was not a one-time thing but a continual process. As Paul said in Romans 12:1–2: "I urge you therefore, brethren, by the mercies of God, to present your bodies a living and holy sacrifice, acceptable to God, which is your spiritual service of worship. And do not be conformed to this world, but be transformed by the renewing of your mind, that you may prove what the will of God is, that which is good and acceptable and perfect" (NAS).

## DAILY MIRACLES

MY SOUTHERN UPBRINGING had led me to believe that God was a Sunday-morning-church phenomenon. But now I was learning that He was with me always—that His presence and power were just as available at the rehabilitation centers and on the streets on Saturday nights (where we did street evangelism regularly) as in church on Sunday morning.

What thrilled me most at Teen Challenge, however, was learning to win souls. I had always looked at Christians as "squares" and "duds." What could possibly be exciting about being good? Then I discovered through the power of the Holy Spirit, I could wage spiritual warfare and be victorious in Christ . . . that "the kingdom of heaven suffers violence, and the violent take it by force" (Matt. 11:12).

Through prayer, we regularly saw God do miracles. Men who were emotionally or physically crippled from all the pain and drugs in their lives were healed. Others diagnosed as manic-depressives and subjected to lifetime sedation were supernaturally delivered. But the greatest miracle was to watch God soften the heart of a street-hardened drug addict before our eyes—to see that person kneel before the Lord in the street and weep tears of joy at finding Christ's forgiveness for the first time as another testimony of God's love. What could possibly be more important, more exciting, than to help change the eternal destiny of a life from hell to heaven, to gain an eternal friend, and win an eternal soul for Jesus? That was the greatest miracle!

For days and weeks, the joy of soul-winning almost burdened me during my rehabilitation program. Why didn't all Christians feel as I did? Why weren't all believers totally dedicated to winning souls? I wondered daily what could possibly be more important? If God could use an ex-burned-out drug addict like me to win souls, surely He could use anyone. Why weren't there more evangelists and missionaries?

Early one morning, I sat on my bed meditating on what had become one of my favorite Scripture passages, Matthew 9:36–38: "When Jesus saw the multitudes, he was moved with compassion on them, because they fainted and were scattered abroad, as sheep having no shepherd. Then saith he unto his disciples, The harvest truly is plenteous, but the laborers are few; pray ye therefore the Lord of the harvest that he will send forth laborers into his harvest."

I prayed the prayer that had been stirring for days in my heart: "Lord, could You possibly use me to reach souls for Your kingdom? If You will do this, I will dedicate my life, my *all* to Your service!"

As I waited and listened for what my God would say, I was almost afraid that I would be rejected. Instead, God's peace and assurance spoke to my heart: "Son, I am your God and I will work in and through you greater things than you can think or imagine, if you remain humble and obedient."

What would the future hold? I had no idea but I knew it had to be exciting!

## A SURE SALVATION

SINCE THAT INCREDIBLE TUESDAY morning in October 1975 and my days at OMA, I've watched God daily work in the lives of people everywhere. Life has become an amazing adventure. In fact, every day I discover more about the love of God and His plan for me. I've been privileged to take the love of God to thousands in the United States and on foreign soil, discovering that the same Jesus Christ who changed my life years ago is alive today. He radically saves and heals on the streets of New York, Chicago, and Los Angeles. The same Holy Spirit who touched me also touches the lives of young and old throughout the United States. The same love of God that penetrated my heart is available to our poverty-stricken neighbors in the slums of Mexico. The same forgiveness that I've received is available for the millions in Canada, Argentina, England, India, Japan, and Africa.

You see, people are the same everywhere. Languages change, customs differ, but the heart is the same in every culture. The Bible says in Jeremiah 17:9 that the human heart is "desperately wicked!" I know from personal experience that only God can change it.

I know also that the love of Jesus Christ can make anyone's life new.

That is why, as I learned during those foundational years at OMA and Teen Challenge—and as I am still learning—every person can be assured of salvation through Jesus Christ. If one is tired, if another is looking for true happiness and peace of mind, if each can relate to some of the heartache and desperation that I felt in my life, all they have to do is follow a few simple steps. They are the same simple steps (and Scriptures) I still share with people who are looking for forgiveness and new life. Anyone who reads them, acts upon them, and allows the love of Jesus Christ to remake him into the person God wants him to be can be saved!

1. *We must believe Christ is our friend, that He cares about us.*

> Casting all your care upon him; for he careth for you.
>
> —1 PETER 5:7

> For we also once were foolish ourselves, disobedient, deceived, enslaved to various lusts and pleasures, spending our life in malice and envy, hateful, hating one another. But when the kindness of God our Savior and His love for mankind appeared, He saved us, not on the basis of deeds which we have done in righteousness, but according to His mercy, by the washing of regeneration and renewing by the Holy Spirit.
>
> —TITUS 3:3–5, NAS

> Henceforth I call you not servants; for the servant knoweth not what his lord doeth: but I have called you friends; for all things that I have heard of my Father I have made known unto you.
>
> —JOHN 15:15

Jesus . . . saith unto them, They that are whole have no need of the physician, but they that are sick: I came not to call the righteous, but sinners to repentance.

—MARK 2:17

For the Son of man is come to save that which was lost.

—MATTHEW 18:11

### 2. *Call on Him for help . . . now!*

For the scripture saith, Whosoever believeth on him shall not be ashamed. For there is no difference between the Jew and the Greek: for the same Lord over all is rich unto all that call upon him. For whosoever shall call upon the name of the Lord shall be saved.

—ROMANS 10:11–13

Come unto me, all ye that labor and are heavy laden, and I will give you rest. Take my yoke upon you, and learn of me; for I am meek and lowly in heart: and ye shall find rest unto your souls. For my yoke is easy, and my burden is light.

—MATTHEW 11:28–30

### 3. *We must believe Him to save us from sin, depression, and fear.*

Verily, verily, I say unto you, He that heareth my word, and believeth on him that sent me, hath everlasting life, and shall not come into condemnation; but is passed from death unto life.

—JOHN 5:24

If thou shalt confess with thy mouth the Lord Jesus,
and shalt believe in thine heart that God hath raised
him from the dead, thou shalt be saved.

—ROMANS 10:9

Who [the Father] hath delivered us from the power
of darkness, and hath translated us into the
kingdom of his dear Son.

—COLOSSIANS 1:13

For God hath not given us the spirit of fear; but of
power, and of love, and of a sound mind.

—2 TIMOTHY 1:7

4. *We must believe that He will cleanse us and
make us over again.*

But if we walk in the light, as he is in the light, we
have fellowship one with another, and the blood of
Jesus Christ his Son cleanseth us from all sin . . . If
we confess our sins, he is faithful and just to forgive
us our sins, and to cleanse us from all unrighteousness.

—1 JOHN 1:7, 9

Therefore if any man be in Christ, he is a new creature: old things are passed away; behold, all things
are become new.

—2 CORINTHIANS 5:17

5. *Confess Him publicly as our Lord and Savior.*

Whosoever therefore shall confess me before men,
him will I confess also before my Father which is in

heaven. But whosoever shall deny me before men, him will I also deny before my Father which is in heaven.

—MATTHEW 10:32–33

Whosoever shall confess that Jesus is the Son of God, God dwelleth in him, and he in God.

—1 JOHN 4:15

For with the heart man believeth unto righteousness; and with the mouth confession is made unto salvation.

—ROMANS 10:10

6. *Trust Him with simple childlike faith.*

And Jesus called a little child unto him, and set him in the midst of them, and said, Verily I say unto you, Except ye be converted, and become as little children, ye shall not enter into the kingdom of heaven.

—MATTHEW 18:2–3

For by grace are ye saved through faith; and that not of yourselves; it is the gift of God.

—EPHESIANS 2:8

But without faith it is impossible to please him: for he that cometh to God must believe that he is, and that he is a rewarder of them that diligently seek him.

—HEBREWS 11:6

That he would grant you, according to the riches of his glory, to be strengthened with might by his Spirit in the inner man; that Christ may dwell in your hearts by faith; that ye, being rooted and grounded in love, may be able to comprehend with all saints what is the breadth, and length, and depth, and height; and to know the love of Christ, which passeth knowledge, that ye might be filled with all the fulness of God. Now unto him that is able to do exceeding abundantly above all that we ask or think, according to the power that worketh in us, unto him be glory.

—EPHESIANS 3:16–21

Therefore being justified by faith, we have peace with God through our Lord Jesus Christ.

—ROMANS 5:1

Over the years, these steps and Scriptures have brought me, and many others, into the light of life. When I think back on those early years in my Christian life, I can't help but thank God. But I also know that I still had much to learn if I was going to see God pour out His Holy Spirit across our land!

*Chapter Four*

# The School of God

*Being confident of this very thing, that he which hath begun a good work in you will perform it until the day of Jesus Christ.*

—Philippians 1:6

WHEN I WAS A STUDENT at Outreach Ministries of Alabama, the rules were strict: no snacking between meals, no leaving beds unmade, that sort of thing. The rules were designed to teach discipline to those of us who were used to doing whatever we wanted, whenever we wanted. As a new Christian, I was just thankful that I hadn't ended up in prison. At least I had the opportunity to learn more about God, even if the structure was more regimented than I was used to. I figured it was probably good for me.

I was assigned to work as a cook. One morning, I rose

early to prepare breakfast for myself and the other guys in the program. Someone had donated a huge sack of flour to us and even though it was riddled with tiny bugs, I still chose to whip up some biscuits and gravy. All the students knew about the tiny, black bugs, and were aware that every biscuit would contain a little extra protein. I had no idea the Holy Spirit was about to use this task to help me deal with an important lesson that would have powerful ramifications throughout my life: How would I allow little or seemingly insignificant sins to affect me?

The smell of fresh-baked biscuits floated through the house as one by one the guys joined me at the table. We talked a bit, ate our breakfast, and prepared for the day's work and study. When we finished and I began to clean up, I noticed that there were two biscuits left over from the meal. My stomach was still a little empty so without even thinking, I reached over, grabbed one, and shoved it into my mouth. No sooner than I began chewing on it did I fall under conviction: I was breaking the rule of no snacking between meals. I looked around, nervously aware of my sin. No one had seen me. But what was I going to do now? I could barely swallow the rest of the biscuit without an enormous sense of guilt descending on me.

Throughout the week, I carried around that guilt like a prisoner would carry around a ball and chain. When I woke in the morning, it was there to greet me. When I worked in the morning, or studied in the afternoon, it came over me. I even had trouble sleeping, all because of one little biscuit! This former thief who had stolen cars, this former drug addict and street urchin who had wreaked havoc everywhere he went, now couldn't get over this little sin of disobeying a rule about eating between meals. God was dealing with me and I knew I had to confess it to my staff leader.

I trembled as I knocked on the door of his office. He motioned me to come in. He told me he had noticed all week that something was bothering me; "How could he help me now?" he asked. He was anticipating a horrendous confession and had braced himself for the worst. All at once, my sin came gushing out. I told him how I had baked the biscuits that morning and shoved one into my mouth after breakfast without even thinking. I confessed to him how all week long the guilt of breaking the rule had bothered me, that I knew I had to take responsibility now for my action.

This gracious, godly man looked down for a minute; I'm sure he was trying hard to suppress a smile. When he looked up, he was as firm as before: "You're right, Steve. You've broken a rule. You're forgiven, but now you still need to suffer the consequence." My punishment? To scrub the kitchen floor with a small brush! I didn't care; I was so happy to be scrubbing rather than carrying around my guilt. I knew I had sinned, and now I was free from the penalty.

Of course, this was a "kindergarten" experience for me in what I call the "school of God." Yet it was one of the first times I remember learning to fear God and obey the rules. I knew He had seen me eat the biscuit, and I was under conviction until I made account for my wrongdoing. He knew if I could learn to be faithful in the little things, I would watch Him do great things in my life.

## PLANTING RIGHTEOUS SEEDS

NOT LONG AFTER MY biscuit-eating episode, I found myself one spring day in the middle of a three-acre garden at the Teen Challenge farm in Missouri. It was a beautiful sunny afternoon. Our schedule included Bible classes in the morning and hard work around the farm in the afternoon. We were divided into work groups: some mowed yards, others tore down buildings to build new ones. My specific task for the next several weeks was to help plant tomatoes, squash, cucumbers, and a variety of other easy-to-grow vegetables.

On this particular day, I was assigned to the garden under the leadership of a staff member who happened to be sixteen years old. He also happened to know virtually nothing about gardening. I was in my early twenties and was well aware of how to treat the soil, how deep to plant the seeds, how to mark the rows, and so on. To me, gardening was a menial task, something that had always come easy for me. I had planted several gardens in Alabama and had eaten of the fruit of my labor—literally.

Then another spiritual test came. My work leader told me to dig holes for the seeds at least a foot deep, and to water them many times daily. My experience told me he was wrong but when I tried to tell him that, he retorted with, "Hey, *I'm* in charge here! Do as I say." I did. As a former drug addict, I could have easily exploded and pounded this young guy into the ground. But I knew I needed to do what he said if I was ever going to learn to please God.

After a few weeks, nothing had grown in the garden. There were no signs of cucumbers, tomatoes, or anything except weeds. The seeds died deep in the ground, and those that had managed to get to the surface were drowned with the over-watering we did. Everyone there was disappointed. My work leader was particularly embarrassed.

What happened next taught me another valuable lesson. My leader came to me one day and apologized for not having listened to me. He went on to say how impressed he was that I had obeyed him anyway, that he saw godly characteristics forming in me, and that he hoped I would forgive him. Of course, I did. This was one of the first opportunities I had to discover what happens when we learn to submit to authority.

Thankfully, I learned early on that we are all in the school of God and no one ever graduates. There are only two ways out: death or the rapture! My biscuit-eating and gardening lessons would seem easy in comparisons to the new level of study I was about to enter.

## MOVING ON

MY THREE MONTHS IN ALABAMA and nine months in Missouri were probably the most memorable of my life. Those boot camp experiences were where I learned the fundamentals of the Christian life: prayer, how to deal with sin, learning my authority over the powers of darkness, developing Christian character. Little compares to those early discoveries.

When I graduated from Teen Challenge, I returned to Outreach Ministries of Alabama for a few months in a reentry program where God allowed me to work in the area of Christian leadership. What a thrilling experience to be used of God in the lives of the new students coming into the program fresh off the streets. Even though I was only a year old in the Lord, I was able to share how a man can indeed be delivered from drugs, alcoholism, and crime, turn his life over to Jesus, and live a holy, fulfilling life.

While actively involved in the ministry of OMA, I received an opportunity that would radically change my future. New York City evangelist David Wilkerson had opened up a Bible school called Twin Oaks Leadership Academy in east Texas and was interviewing twenty-five male and twenty-five female students to attend that academic year. A representative from Twin Oaks was travelling throughout the United States interviewing Teen Challenge graduates to fill these few spots. They were offering an all-expenses paid, two-year Bible-college experience for prospective Christian leaders. The school was set up in two phases: one year of academic, classroom instruction would be followed by one year of on-the-job training. I applied, and to my astonishment, I was picked.

Twin Oaks Leadership Academy, now a recognized Bible training center, would be the next phase for me in the school of God. It was there that I learned the fundamentals of Christian leadership. For one year of intense study, I was prepared by godly men and women whom David Wilkerson brought in as instructors. For instance, Leonard Ravenhill taught on prayer; Nicky Cruz taught a special class on evangelism. (Nicky, a former gang leader, had been won to Christ by David Wilkerson on the streets of New York.) A host of other seasoned men and women of God taught on a variety of necessary attributes for effective ministry. We even had a class on etiquette. I'll never forget how comical it was to watch our teacher discuss the proper use of salad forks, soup spoons, and tea cups. Most of us were from the streets and ate more like animals than humans.

I was involved in the school music ensemble, led by Tim and LaDonna Johnson, who were part of the Christian singing group, Dallas Holm and Praise. Dallas, along with his band, lived on campus. What an incredible atmosphere in which to learn about Jesus. Just down the street was Last Days Ministries. Keith Green, it's founder, periodically joined us for lunch in our cafeteria. We were also blessed to frequently attend his free concerts for the locals.

Twin Oaks was a beautiful campus, with several lakes nestled throughout the four-hundred-acre ranch. In order to compensate for our tuition fees, all of the students were assigned job duties around the property. During the mornings, we went through the academic program and in the afternoons we would work at some job like grounds upkeep, office work, or gardening.

Early in the school year I noticed that several students had been dismissed from the academy, and various rumors had filtered around about why they were gone. None of us knew then that these students had broken some of the most basic rules. For instance, we were required to maintain a personal quiet time, we could not come and go as we pleased, lights had to be out by 10 P.M., and, above all, there was absolutely no dating.

After seeing these students get kicked out, I determined in my heart to become the most serious student on campus. No matter what, I was not going to allow anything to sidetrack my goal of completing the year at the top of my class. But even my newfound determination could not prevent the inevitable from happening.

## LOVELY DISTRACTIONS

MY JOB AT TWIN OAKS ACADEMY was to run errands. In essence, I was the gopher; I had to go for this and go for that. I was given a small orange Datsun pick-up truck and regularly would be responsible for picking up supplies in Tyler or Dallas, Texas. Often that meant I would have to go to the main business office to pick up a check and to find out what errands needed to be completed for the day.

The secretary working in the main office was a beautiful Christian woman in her early twenties named Jeri Larson. Each time I walked through the door, I could not help but notice her. We talked a little more each time I was there, and soon I found myself looking forward to going to the main office. Before I knew it, what I feared the most had come upon me. My absolute determination not to allow anything to deter me from my academic goals was now being challenged by a lovely distraction, a love-at-first-sight experience.

As hard as I tried (and believe me, I tried hard through prayer, Scripture memorization, and fasts), I could not get Jeri off my mind. As a matter of fact, the more I tried, the more the struggle increased. Finally, the struggle being too great to bear, I confessed my love-struck burden to one of the leaders. He said he wasn't shocked; in fact, he said he "knew it all along." Still, he reminded me of the rules, and I assured him that I had no intention of breaking them.

A short while later (unbeknown to me), Jeri came into the same leader's office and confessed that she, too, had fallen in love. She had tried her very best to shake it, she told him, but "this guy named Steve" had won her heart. Our leader reminded her, too, of the rules. But he was beginning to realize that God was indeed putting Jeri and me together.

He called me back into his office a short time later and instructed me that I would be allowed to meet with Jeri for fifteen minutes three times a week. He confirmed to me that God might be putting us together, so he gave us rigid rules to follow. There would be absolutely no public displays of affection, no hand-holding, no hugging, no kissing, nothing that might cause others (or ourselves) to stumble as we began building a relationship.

Today, it is mind-boggling to think that these two former street kids who were used to doing what they wanted were now being told exactly how they could interact with the opposite sex. Someone else might have told these leaders, "Who do you think you are, trying to run my life? I am, after all, an adult." But I was learning . . . again . . . that if I would be faithful with the small things God would bless me with bigger things.

Neither Jeri nor I resisted the instructions our leaders gave us concerning our relationship. If anything, we both rejoiced that we could submit to our authorities, a true testimony that only God could have changed our lives. We remained obedient in every way, and made the most of our three meetings a week. We talked about all sorts of things, prayed together, and dreamed about the future. As a result, I fell in love with Jeri as a spiritual woman. She fell in love with me as a spiritual man. To this day, I am convinced that when there is no physical contact, when two people have to talk with each other, it is amazing the depth of love they can experience with each other. I realized that the conditions our leaders put on us weren't just for our own good, but were for God's best!

Finally, I knew the day had come to ask Jeri for her hand in marriage. We were just a few months from graduation, and there was no doubt in my mind by this time that God had put us together. As we were taking one of our fifteen-minute walks, strolling down the fence-line surrounding (of all things), a cow pasture, I stopped and turned to Jeri. "I want to ask you something." She looked into my eyes as I asked, "Jeri, will you marry me? Will you be my wife?"

She smiled, and whispered, "How could I say no?"

We laughed as we heard the cows mooing at the same moment she said yes; it had to be a confirmation! At such an occasion, most couples would have embraced and kissed. But we were still under rules and regulations. So I said something corny like, "Wow, that's great!" And we walked separately back to our dorms.

Two months later, we both graduated from Twin Oaks at the top of our class. God had honored our faithfulness. We had accepted positions with OMA back in Alabama, where a year after graduation we were married. Our courtship and our leadership training were incredible experiences, laying for us a firm foundation in the work God had called us to do together.

Today, I am so thankful that I learned early in my Christian life the joys of submitting to authority and the attributes of self-control and godly contentment. To this day, I believe God has put everyone of us under authorities to help form in us Christian character. It is part of His schooling. If we keep running from authority, how can iron sharpen iron? That is also why I am such a firm believer of the importance of being active members of a local Bible-believing church. We need His structure.

## BUSY FOR GOD

THE FIRST FEW YEARS of our married lives, Jeri and I found ourselves in a flurry of Christian activities. I was wearing several hats: evangelist, youth pastor, producer of evangelistic-Christian festivals and concerts, counselor, and, of course, husband. Jeri worked with me in many of these events, and we were thrilled at the opportunities to enter another exciting level in God's school. Eventually, I moved into the role of missionary as well.

During a three-year tenure as a youth pastor of Evangel Assembly of God in Tallahassee, Florida, we organized our first-ever missions trip to Mexico. I will never forget the impact that trip had on me. One experience in particular convinced me of the importance of reaching the lost with the Good News of Jesus.

I was holding a box of tracts on a street corner in

downtown Mexico City, watching people come by and take the tracts. Observing these hungry souls come by for spiritual food tugged heavily on my heart. Soon, I began to cry. I watched them take the tracts and go lean against the wall of a building to read about the love of Jesus, many for the first time in their lives. At that point, I believe God spoke to me about missions, about the millions who have not yet had the opportunity to hear about the love of Christ, as compared to so many who had heard of Him but rejected the invitation.

On another day during this short-term missions trip, we decided to take a break and visit the pyramids. While the others enjoyed the tourist site, I began talking with a man named Don Exley, who just happened to be a missionary from Argentina. He had been working for one year in Mexico City. As we talked, I told him of my new desire to become a missionary, of the tears I had cried for the lost on that street corner. I admitted that I wasn't sure where God was leading me; I just knew I needed to be a missionary for Him.

He listened intently as I shared. Then, quietly and with unmistakable authority, he looked at me and said, "Steve, if you make up your mind to become a missionary, please consider Argentina." Little did he know the impact of his challenge; a seed was planted that day that God would water and nurture. Fourteen months later, Jeri and I found ourselves in San Jose, Costa Rica, as ordained Assembly of God missionaries at the Institute of Languages, an independent language-training school. Our long-range plans were to minister in Argentina!

In language school, we learned the importance of cross-cultural communication. We became convinced that the best way to learn the language was to live with the Costa Ricans. So one day, Jeri and I boarded a city bus and went from seat to seat, asking people in our best broken Spanish this question: "We are living in Costa Rica to learn Spanish and need to practice what we learn. Can we live with you?"

Many said, "Sí, como no" which means, "Sure, why not?" But when we followed up, we found many did not have the room for us.

Eventually, we found one family who was willing, and able, to take us in. We ate beans and rice with them and watched them barter in the market. What an experience, what a valuable education that was! I found it so much easier to reach the Costa Ricans with the gospel once I experienced how they lived. This was another wonderful chapter in the life of a student enrolled in the school of God!

## HEADING SOUTH

AFTER WE GRADUATED FROM language school, Jeri and I went immediately to Buenos Aires, Argentina, to begin work in church-planting and evangelism. I visited Argentina a month before we had gone to Costa Rica. During that first trip to Argentina, I had an experience that would deeply shape my perspective of evangelism.

I was in the city of Mar Del Plata, a bustling city on the Atlantic coast, rich in tourism, similar in many ways to Las Vegas. I decided to visit an evangelistic campaign held by the renowned evangelist, Carlos Annacondia. The campaign was being held in an open city park; I had heard the event was drawing fifteen- to twenty-thousand people. I had to see this for myself. How could so many people be hungry for the truth of God's love?

A friend had shared with Carlos my testimony, and to my surprise, I was given an opportunity to speak to the huge crowd. I will never forget the spiritual hunger reflected on the people's faces. They hung on every word as I shared my testimony. I told them how God had delivered me from a life of drug addiction and crime, how He had changed my heart and taught me many things about His forgiveness and new life.

But I was completely unprepared for what happened when I left the platform. The people stormed me, crying out for a touch from "the man of God." One lady grabbed my hand, turned it around, touched her forehead, and fell immediately to the ground. I was stunned. When I saw what happened to her, I began touching the foreheads of the other people. They were immediately thrown to the ground. I was shocked at what was happening and thrilled to be used by God to touch their lives. I felt like God's man for the hour as I slipped through the crowd praying for people.

About twenty minutes into the experience, the crusade manager came up to me and told me to stop what I was doing. He wisely took me aside and said, "These people are so hungry for God, anyone can do what you're doing. They saw you on the platform and recognized you as a man of God. We don't pray with people until the conclusion of the service. Please submit to our rules." I was immediately humbled. Even though this was obviously a mighty move of the Holy Spirit, I knew I had to submit to the crusade's rules and gladly did so.

A few hours later, I listened as the evangelist gave an altar call. Again, I was unprepared for what I was about to witness: I watched several thousand Argentines literally run forward to Jesus. I then saw something I had never seen before. Carlos waved his hand across the crowd and began speaking to sicknesses, diseases, demons, witches, and anything else that might have bound the people. He called out cancer and rebuked it; he called out alcoholism and drug addiction and rebuked it. People again started falling to the ground. Reports came in of people who were simply walking by the crusade site, perhaps to buy an ice-cream cone, and were overcome by the power of God. It was uncanny the authority this man of God had over the powers of darkness. He was operating in a realm with the masses that was unfamiliar to me. Yes, I had been used by God to cast some demons out and to bind some devils, but nothing of this magnitude. I knew then I was about to enter the next grade in the school of God.

For the next seven years, we ministered in Argentina. Those years were filled with fiery evangelistic meetings, church planting, one-on-one soul-winning, praying for the sick, and everything else a committed missionary is called on to do. One of the most memorable experiences in our lives was the opportunity we had to build an orphanage in San Nicolas, a city outside Buenos Aires. Jeri and I visited the orphanage in 1984, and wept over the horrendous conditions there. Under the loving care of their adopted father, Carlos Naranjo, the children were clothed, fed, and housed, but he never had sufficient funds to meet all their needs. Through a series of miracles too numerous to mention, we were able to construct a beautiful, one hundred-bed orphanage. It was a combined effort of many concerned Christians—every detail was taken care of. David Wilkerson's ministry bought new bunk beds for the kids, and a group of women came down from the States to sew and hang the curtains. Someone said, "These kids are moving from a pig-pen to a palace." Carlos wrote in his book, before he died, that we were his angels, sent from God.

I saw with my own eyes the incredible ways Jesus drew people to His heart, changed their lives, and healed their communities. The Lord placed around me some powerful young men of God, such as Hector Ferreyra, who diligently labored alongside us in the field. Together, we saw thousands of people saved and planted several churches in Southern Argentina. God's call for me to reach the lost was becoming clearer. I began to feel the burden for other areas of the world.

## GLOBAL LESSONS

MY EVANGELISTIC ZEAL carried me from Argentina to Colombia, Spain, Russia, Chile, Uruguay, and several other areas around the world. God opened the doors for me to be able to plant churches in Colombia, Spain, and Russia, and hold evangelistic crusades in these other places. Many times there were not even local churches there to work with. Yet, God always provided and worked in miraculous ways to bring people together to accomplish His purposes.

Each of these experiences, just like the experiences in everyone else's lives, were chapters for me as I learned about Christ and His love for people, His design for man, His longing for the lost. I could write so much more about these places, and maybe someday I will. But for now I know that each of these missionary experiences taught me a little more about what God was calling me to do.

In fact, as I look back on these times, I see different seasons of my life—times when I was rigid and not open to God, times when I was more teachable. I can see how I learned the importance of being open to the Holy Spirit and yielding to Him in that moment. In other words, I discovered church-planting in Argentina is simply not the same as it is in Russia. I had to learn to discern from the Holy Spirit what was best in each situation.

I want to remain flexible and pliable in the hands of the Potter. Just as in Acts 18:24–28, Apollos, an eloquent speaker, learned to be open to the instruction from Aquila and Priscilla, I, too, have learned to be open to whatever God has in store for me and for those around me.

And, in retrospect, I have even begun to realize how each level of training for me around the world prepared me for a mighty outpouring of God's Spirit in a little town called Pensacola, Florida.

*Chapter Five*

# A Father's Day Surprise

*O Lord, I have heard thy speech, and was afraid; O Lord, revive thy work in the midst of the years, in the midst of the years make known; in wrath remember mercy.*

—HABAKKUK 3:2

I CALLED PASTOR John Kilpatrick of Brownsville Assembly of God early one morning in May 1995 as a follow-up to a conversation we had not long before. As a missionary evangelist, I am constantly in need of financial and prayerful support for mission projects and church plants throughout the world. I had called Pastor Kilpatrick six months earlier from Belarus in the former Soviet Union to tell him of the exciting work God was doing there; he responded by committing to us a large sum of money for our work. Several months had gone by, and the money still had not been deposited in my account. Little did I know that my phone call that spring morning would drastically change our destinies.

We never did talk about money. We had known each other for over twelve years and had always found ourselves discussing the deeper things of God, even when the intention of the call was otherwise. From the moment our conversation began, our hearts were knit together discussing not finances, or even our mission work. Instead we talked about revival. On the other end, I heard a man craving a fresh touch from God.

I shared with Pastor Kilpatrick what I had seen God doing around the world. I explained to him how I was experiencing a personal revival in my own life and how my family had been affected as well. I shared about the churches I had been privileged to visit throughout the world, churches touched by the power of God. I will never forget his response:

"Steve, I want you to come now, as quickly as you can."

I looked at my calendar; it was booked throughout the year. I was scheduled to preach in churches throughout the United States as well as with crusades in Colombia, Russia, and Czechoslovakia. I had absolutely no dates available. I apologized to my friend, frustrated that I was not able to help him. Wasn't there anything I could do? When I glanced one more time at my packed agenda, I did notice one lone Sunday that was not yet marked.

"Father's Day is the only Sunday available this year," I told him, almost certain that he would not want me to come that day.

No pastor allows a visiting speaker to preach on Father's Day. Why? It is a time for the congregation to be together and to honor the local men of their church community. It is a day of exhortation and recognition for the fathers of the year, where often the youngest father and the oldest father are recognized. Families then celebrate the remainder of the day together with a good meal and fellowship. *There's no way,* I thought, *that John Kilpatrick will be interested in me preaching on Father's Day. Besides, it's only two weeks away.*

"I want you to be with us on Father's Day, Steve," John said clearly over the phone lines. "Come for the evening service. Please."

I agreed.

## FATHER KNOWS BEST

TWO WEEKS LATER when I arrived in Pensacola, John asked me to preach not only on Sunday night but to share from the Word on Father's Day morning as well. An uneasiness came over me as I thought of what the congregation may be anticipating from their pastor. Could I meet their expectations? Would they be satisfied with a visiting evangelist sharing a message from his heart rather than a word of encouragement from their pastor? But I agreed after John shared with me how difficult his week had been.

He had lost his mother shortly before and had just endured one of the most excruciating weeks in his ministry. Though he had been praying for over two years that God would send revival to his church, he was exhausted. In fact, I had visited his church not long before during a Sunday night service as his congregation prayed for revival. I was astonished at their intensity in seeking God for revival. But now I could see that their pastor was tired. As a friend and a partner in ministry, I reluctantly chose to preach that Sunday morning, praying that our heavenly Father knew what He was doing. Of course, He did. His ways are always best.

The next morning my awkward feeling was even more intensified when Pastor Kilpatrick asked me not to sit on the platform but in the pews. He would call me up when it was time to preach. He was afraid of how the congregation would respond seeing a visiting preacher on the platform. Due to his mother's long-term illness, Pastor Kilpatrick had asked several visiting preachers to fill in for him. Now the members were anxious to hear from their own pastor. I had known for years that the congregation at Brownsville deeply loved their pastor and respected his authority. So I wasn't sure what would happen next.

That Sunday-morning Father's Day service started out in a typical way: We sang a few choruses and hymns, took the offering, recognized the Father of the Year, and also celebrated with one long-time Brownsville member, Marc Baker, a father whose wife had just had quintuplets—four boys and one girl. There was an atmosphere of celebration and gratitude for strong family values. My anxiety level began to diminish when the pastor introduced me, recalling the several times before when I had preached at Brownsville and had been well received. I sensed God at work.

## SHARPENING OUR MEMORY

I SPOKE THAT DAY ON Psalm 77:11–12: "I will remember the works of the Lord: surely I will remember thy wonders of old. I will meditate also of all thy work, and talk of thy doings." The message had to do with remembering all that the Lord had done in our lives, and how important it is in facing the battles of the future to go back to the victories of the past. I spoke of my radical conversion experience, remembering how the Lord had graciously set me free from the bondage of sin and drug abuse, and how God had later allowed me to be around some great and wonderful men of God like Leonard Ravenhill.

I recalled how just a few months before, as Leonard lay in a coma, preparing to meet Jesus, I went to visit him in his home. I leaned over and whispered to him, "Leonard, Jeri's pregnant. We're going to have a baby!" Though this great man was in a deep coma, he squeezed my hand when he heard my news! I will never forget it. God had brought me through the difficult time of losing one my most significant spiritual mentors by helping me remember His wonders, the miracle of new life.

As I was preaching that morning in Brownsville, I felt in my spirit an unexplainable sense of gratitude, thankful for how God had guided my life, called me out of darkness, and brought me to this point on this Father's Day. I talked about how important it is to remember how faithfully God has delivered us from difficult situations in the past, such as sicknesses, financial crises, or family problems.

It feeds our faith when we speak of the things He has done. Because even though we are children of God, sometimes we forget all that He has done for us.

I even found myself sharing with the congregation about the great Argentine revival that Jeri and I had been a part of for seven years. It came alive again in my spirit, just as it comes alive to me any time we speak of our salvation or of God's glorious works. When I spoke of the times of visitations from the Lord, of the different seasons of revival, my own spirit was exhorted and refreshed.

I continued the sermon by citing the powerful truth of Hebrews 13:8, "Jesus Christ the same yesterday, and today, and forever." It is so important to understand that what God did in the past, He still can do today. The miracles He performed yesterday He can perform today. The signs and wonders of the Bible are just as real today!

## TRANSFORMING A CYNIC

ABOUT THIS TIME I FELT a sense of anticipation from the congregation. They hung on every word and seemed genuinely anxious to receive a fresh touch from God. I shared with them how I knew the Lord wanted to pour out His Spirit on all of us, that He desired for us to be refreshed and renewed. I shared with them how the Wednesday before the Lord had spoken to me as I was mowing my yard (sometimes God talks to us in the strangest places). The Lord had told me: "Everyone in the service on Sunday, every single person who is spiritually dry will be drenched with a heavenly rain."

First, I knew I needed to explain what had happened to me during a recent visit to an Anglican church in London, England. I shared how God had set me free from a critical spirit. I had become cynical, but He refreshed my heart and brought me into a new dimension of His love. I explained how I sensed the nearness of Jesus throughout each day of that trip in ways I had never before experienced.

What happened in London? It began when someone handed me a *Time* magazine article about a fresh move of God in the churches in England. I had received this article from a friend while we were working together in Russia. As I read it, I had to admit my curiosity was aroused, although I had been extremely critical toward any of the current "moves" of God throughout the world. I was turned off by reports of a "laughing" movement and was unimpressed by stories of people falling to the ground. As a missionary evangelist, I was always the one who said, "I don't care if you shake, fall, or tremble, but I do want to see you changed." Being a church planter, I was always concerned about lasting fruit. I considered anything else to be a waste of time.

# A Father's Day Surprise

To me, all that was taking place around the world under the title of "renewal" was superficial and shallow. I had become calloused to any positive statements concerning this contemporary "renewal." As a matter of fact, a friend from Prague had called and asked me what I thought of the movement. I told him I thought it was nothing more than brainwashing and mind-control. (Sure, I had seen manifestations of the Holy Spirit in Argentina but it was always in the context of church-planting and evangelism, bearing lasting fruit for God's kingdom.) To me, if people weren't getting saved and falling under a deep conviction of sin, what good was it if they fell to the ground?

Still, I could not help but wonder what was happening with the English. What in the world would these well-respected, proper, and stoic countrymen be doing falling to the ground, risking looking foolish? I knew in my spirit that there had to be something to it, so I decided to investigate. Besides, a visit to London meant the opportunity to add to my extensive library more rare old Christian books. For years, I have lived in constant search of classic Christian literature, specifically on revival; England had always provided me with such treasures. Going there again would give me a two-fold purpose: to find Christian books and to find out what was happening within the Anglican church.

That morning in Brownsville, I shared with the people my London experiences. My missionary team and I had been in Frankfurt and decided to rent a car and drive to London. We planned to cross the English Channel by ferry. While on the ferry, something happened that indicated to me that God was about to do something powerful in my life in London.

As we were crossing the channel, I looked out at the beautiful white cliffs of Dover. They were majestic and beautiful. Directly behind them appeared a rainbow, and it was pointing toward London. I was astonished at the beauty of the rainbow, so I pulled out my camera to take a picture. While my camera was focused on the rainbow, I was deeply moved by what happened next: the bagpipes of Scotland playing the most beautiful rendition of "Amazing Grace" I had ever heard came over the ferry intercom loud and clear! This was not a Christian cruise line. This was a secular ferry playing "Amazing Grace" on Scottish bagpipes. Tears welled in my eyes and I knew God had something special for me in London.

Our time in London was limited, and consumed by visiting old book shops, touring Christian landmarks such as John Wesley's home and church, and finally, walking into Holy Trinity Brompton Cathedral. It was raining hard as I entered the church. I was astonished to see at least five hundred English men and women seeking God on that cold, damp afternoon. I looked around the magnificent cathedral and noticed that some people were crying, some were moaning or groaning, and a few were laughing. But overall, there was an undeniable presence of the Most Holy God. I knew without a doubt that this was a visitation of God, and I was determined not to miss it.

## A Touch from Heaven

THROUGH A FRIEND, I had made an appointment with the vicar of Holy Trinity, Reverend Sandy Millar. But when I entered the church, I knew that this present move of God was not about *talking*. It was about *receiving*. I was so tired of being critical and cynical, so tired of pride and arrogance, so tired of listening to everyone—including myself—degrade other men's ministries. All I wanted was a fresh touch from God.

I told Sandy I didn't think it was necessary to talk.

Instead I asked if he could just lay hands on me and pray. He agreed. As he did, he quietly and simply said, "Touch him, Jesus. Bless him, Lord." When I heard the sound of his prayer, something strange happened. My bodily strength left immediately, and I fell to the ground. This same experience had happened to me in Argentina under the ministry of Carlos Annacondia. But what happened next was different.

I sensed the nearness of Jesus in a powerful way, a way that I had not experienced since that October day when I first called on His name. It was as if He had poured fresh water over my dry, thirsty soul. Sandy got down on the floor with me and said these words to me: "You don't have to do anything. He loves you. Rest in that love. Nurture that love. From that will come the harvest. Don't try to *do* anything. You don't have to prove anything to anybody."

I knew that my life would never be the same. I was washed clean of my critical spirit and felt an over-whelming love for the whole body of Christ in all her unique denominations: Anglicans, Episcopalians, Presby-terians, Pentecostals, Baptists, Methodists, and so on. My time in England provided me with more than just trea-sured books; I was renewed in a powerful way that left me hungry for more of God.

All this I shared with the congregation in Brownsville that Father's Day in 1995. As I stared into the faces of these friends, I detected the same determination to shake loose of stale, dry religion. I could sense that these people wanted a fresh move of God like I had experienced in England. I knew God would not disappoint us.

An altar call was given that Father's Day for those who had never received the Lord or those who had wandered from Jesus. A few minutes later I gave a second call, saying "I want to pray with anyone who wants a fresh touch from

God." To our astonishment, one thousand people came forward for that second altar call.

Later, I learned that when John Kilpatrick saw this response, he mumbled under his breath, "Dear God, we're going to be here all day praying for these people!" After all, it was Father's Day. It was almost time to go eat lunch with the family, not spend hours at the altar. But the heart of another cynic was being transformed that day as well!

## THE RAIN FALLS

PASTOR KILPATRICK BEGRUDGINGLY joined me at the altar as his congregation came forward for prayer. We prayed together for each man or woman, as the choir and congregation sang that familiar chorus, "The Name of the Lord is a strong tower. The righteous run into it and they are saved."

Within seconds, we knew something amazing was breaking forth that day in the church. The power of God exploded at the altar! It was as if the hunger on the people's faces drew the presence of God, much as dry soil attracts water. Even Pastor Kilpatrick was touched mightily by God and lay immobilized for over three hours, drinking in the presence of God! (Later, he told me the Lord was supernaturally draining from him all the stress he had held from the previous months in ministry.) It became obvious to me that we were at the beginning of a wonderful and Holy visitation that would last for more than one service.

As in revivals of old, people fell on their knees, prostrate or backward on the ground, weeping and wailing and crying out to God. John and I prayed for individuals, and I realized that repentance was on the hearts of these people. I heard them cry out to God about their lukewarmness and stale Christianity, confessing their sins, and wanting desperately to get right with God. It seemed that everyone in that sanctuary desired a renewed relationship with their Lord Jesus Christ. And God was responding.

We never made it to lunch that day. As a matter of fact, I did not get back to my hotel until 4:30 P.M. and immediately began preparing for the evening service at six o'clock. I expected the evening service to be a continuation of what happened that afternoon. It was. I preached a message on the importance of being desperate for God, and the altars again were flooded.

Around midnight, John Kilpatrick turned to me and said, "Steve, I think we need to go another day."

I said, "Let's ask the people."

Their response was a unanimous and enthusiastic yes!

Little did we know that a prophecy the Lord gave Dr. David Yonggi Cho back in 1991 was about to come to pass. (Dr. Cho is pastor of the world's largest church in Seoul Korea.) Here is Dr. Cho's prophetic word:

> When I was ministering in Seattle, Washington, in 1991, I became deeply concerned about the spiritual decline in America. I began to pray even more earnestly for revival in these United States. As I prayed, I felt the Lord prompt me to get a map of America, and to point my finger on the map. I found myself pointing to the city of Pensacola in the Florida panhandle.
>
> Then I sensed the Lord say, "I am going to send revival to the seaside city of Pensacola, and it will spread like a fire until all of America has been consumed by it."

The next day, my wife, son, daughter, and new baby girl

were flown in from Texas for what we all thought would be an extended revival that would last only a short while.

We were wrong.

*Chapter Six*

# Searchlights

*Search me, O God, and know my heart: try me, and know my thoughts: And see if there me any wicked way in me, and lead in the way everlasting.*

—Psalm 139:23–24

R EVIVAL FELL ON JUNE 18, 1995. We had expected it to last for a few nights. But the nights turned into weeks, the weeks into months, and the months into two years. It's still going, as of this writing. God surprised us with His wonderful, powerful presence, and as a result, many, many people will never be the same. A holy expectancy infuses us each night as we lift up the name of Jesus, wait on Him, and watch the Spirit of the living God move in ways few of us could imagine.

Many reporters have come to the revival services, and each reporter communicates the same thing: *Something extraordinary is happening in Pensacola.* Yes, they notice the thousands of people waiting in line for nightly services. They discover that many have come from across the world, from places like Japan, Uganda, Scotland, Germany, Australia, Ontario, and from every state in the United States. They observe the lively worship, the preaching, and the prayer time. But mostly they recognize that these people are humble and broken, and that somehow their lives are being changed. Journalists from Christian publications identify it for what it is: *repentance.* Secular journalists are baffled at the positive response of so many baby-boomers and generation X-ers. One such journalist asked me why thousands of young people flock to Brownsville Assembly. My response was simple: "They are hungry for truth, and nothing or no one satisfies them like Jesus."

I believe God will not move in the lives of His people until they first lay their lives at His feet, asking Him to search their hearts as they repent of their selfish ways. I have watched over and over again as God's people desperately want Him to show them their wicked ways, to transform their lives, to search their hearts. Such searching requires a Holy searchlight. And I am so thankful to God for His light that has continually shown on us, night after night at the Brownsville revival.

## EXPOSING WICKEDNESS

NOT LONG AGO, A PASTOR from another state attended several of our services. Brother Martin (we'll call him) told me later that week that he could not believe the intensity of the revival services. The tall, dark-haired pastor came to Brownsville from the Midwest to watch and observe the meetings. He wanted to glean what he could in hopes of taking "it" back home so his own congregation could experience revival. Brother Martin patiently watched and prayed each night; he knew sinners were being saved, and he expected that. But he had no idea that God would grip his own heart and shine a light on areas where he himself needed cleansing.

"Last night I called my wife, Brother Steve," he told me. I listened to the shaky voice of this otherwise intelligent, sincere man. He paused, broken at what he was about to share with me. Tears filled his eyes. He recalled how he told his wife to go to the video cabinet and dispose of any videos that contained curse words or lewd scenes that would grieve the Holy Spirit. "I explained to her how it would be impossible to have revival in our own lives and in the lives of our own church members if we didn't first deal with the root problem of sin." He told me he also contacted all the deacons of his four hundred-member church to do likewise. They agreed and began to clean house. I listened intently to his commitment. I encouraged him to stand firm and reminded him that without holiness no man will see the Lord. Brother Martin left Pensacola with a new vision of holiness and revival for his church.

Brother Martin is just one example of the type of behavior that has been a consistent part of the Brownsville revival from the very beginning. It is sheer hypocrisy for any of us to want an anointing from God while holding on to besetting sins. In fact, many Christians today remind me of Simon the Sorcerer in the Book of Acts who wanted to buy the power of the Holy Ghost. That attitude says to me, "We want a little bit of God and a little bit of the world." Yet, if we are honest with ourselves and with God, we will have to admit that it just doesn't work that way.

That is why during most revival nights, I try my very best to arrive at the church early in order to meet with visiting pastors, evangelists, and church leaders from around the world. Then I notice that when I meet with them later on in the revival week, our conversations seem to be deeper, and they seem a bit more broken, humbled even. There is no doubt this is due to a number of things: the intense preaching against sin to which they have been subjected the nights before, the spirit of worship, and the attitude of humility and vulnerability before the Lord. From beginning to end, the revival services have a way of breaking past the superficiality of our lives. Those who are willing to examine their hearts and become teachable receive a fresh touch from God. I've seen it time and again.

Each revival service is a time of serious self-examination and personal evaluation. In every service sinners who have never known the Lord come running under conviction to the altar. The Holy Spirit has a way of shining His gentle but piercing light into the darkness in their lives, and they are found pleading to the Lord for forgiveness.

Just as David pleaded with God in Psalm 139 for a holy life, so, too, must we plead for such an examination time. In essence, David gave the Lord permission to search his life thoroughly; those who come to the revival do the same. Each of us can do no less.

## COMING ABOARD

LET'S ONCE AGAIN READ these precious verses from Psalm 139. As we do, I've included a few explanatory words or phrases which I believe can help us better understand what David was trying to say:

Search me [examine me thoroughly], O God, and

know [recognize, observe with instruction even to the point of punishment if needed] my heart: try me [prove me, put me to the test, allow me to face trials], and know my thoughts [my inner man, those things hidden to others]: and see if there be any wicked way in me [idolatrous, anything that takes the place of You in my life], and lead me in the way everlasting [the vanishing point, when this life ceases to exist and I am eternally with You].

A good illustration for this passage can be seen in the navy's vernacular phrase, "Right of Search." The Right of Search is the right claimed by one nation to authorize the commanders of their ships to enter vessels of other nations. When they do, they can examine their papers and cargo to determine the character of the vessel and the destination of the cargo. For instance, if a foreign vessel floats into U.S. territorial waters, the U.S. Navy has the right to pull up alongside to examine the ship's papers, and if necessary, commence a search to determine whether or not the ship should be allowed to continue.

All of us—those attending the revival and those reading this book—are like ships floating into the Lord's waters. He is pulling up alongside and saying, "I would like to come aboard." In the process, He is inherently asking us to search our hearts—the hulls of our ships, so to speak.

God is not in the business of playing games. If we want Jesus Christ to truly work in our lives, we must yield to Him, giving Him complete lordship. People say to me all the time, "I want God to work in my life."

*Oh really,* I say to myself. Then I ask, "Are you willing to let God have total control? Are you willing for Him to search you even when it means relinquishing those things that are hidden deep down in the inner recesses of your heart?" The question for each of us is: "Am I willing to let Him shine a light on every area of my life?"

Often the answer is *no*. We do not really want God to touch those secret areas. It is too uncomfortable, too painful. But we must remember there are no secrets with God. Jesus saw the pain of the man who stood begging at the edge of the healing waters, and still asked him, "Do you want to be healed?" Jesus was able to see into the depths of the man's situation. First Samuel 16:7 also declares this truth: "For the Lord seeth not as man seeth; for man looketh on the outward appearance, but the Lord looketh on the heart."

Leonard Ravenhill used to say to me, "So, Stevie, do you really want to be like Jesus? Do you want to spend forty days in fasting and prayer? Do you want a Gethsemane? Do you want a Judas in your life? Do you want a doubting Thomas? Do you want a friend who spent three years with you to curse and insist he never knew you? Do you want God to dissolve your social life?" These probing questions shine a whole new light on the true call to Christian discipleship.

## A HOLY SPOTLIGHT

AS A RESULT, I BELIEVE there are three different types of searches that we allow to happen in our lives. They come up often at revival. Two of these searches are basically worthless. The last reveals the hidden secrets of the heart and when completed brings about true fulfillment. I call these three searches:

1. The surface search
2. The spot search
3. The cellar search

I tell friends who visit the revival, "Before venturing into these waters, it is important to first establish a few facts about the One doing the searching, the One who wants to climb aboard ship."

I love how John Flavel, the Puritan writer, put it in his *A Treatise on Keeping the Heart,* in the 1600s:

> "The One searching is God and He does not want to harm you. God's intention is not to hurt you but to heal you. You lie too near His heart for Him to hurt you. Nothing grieves Him more than your groundless and unworthy suspicions of His designs. Consider these examples:
>
> Would it grieve a tender-hearted physician if the patient screamed out, 'He's trying to *kill* me!' upon taking the prescribed medicine or feeling the pain of an operation?
>
> Marines in a storm can throw overboard the most valuable goods to preserve their lives.
>
> Armies will destroy fine buildings throughout a city just to keep the enemy from hiding in them.
>
> Those who have had gangrene or a severe case of frostbite on a part of their body, have not only had the limb cut off, but paid the doctor."[1]

Yes, the One searching is God, and He does not want to harm us. He searches through preaching, trials, temptations, persecutions, and of course, He searches through the lives of other people. His searchlight is the truth of the Word of God. "For the Word of God is quick, and powerful, and sharper than any two edged sword, piercing even to the dividing asunder of soul and spirit, and of the joints and marrow, and is a discerner of the thoughts and intents of the heart. Neither is there any creature that is not manifest in his sight: but all things are naked and opened unto the eyes of him with whom we have to do" (Heb. 4:12–13). The Word of God is not only a probing instrument, as Hebrews 4 says, but a devouring flame (Jer. 5:14), a crushing hammer (Jer. 23:29), a lamp, and a light (Ps. 119:105).

When performing His search, God uses a high-intensity halogen spotlight, not a penlight with worn-out AAA batteries. His purposes are to expose sin and cleanse us from all wickedness. His cleansing agent is the Holy Ghost, and the results are purity and eternal life with Him! There's no use searching for shelter; we cannot hide from God's searchlight. We cannot hide from the God who loves us so much that He gave His Son in our stead. That is the message at the heart of any revival—personal or corporate.

Now we know there are times when God will come aboard whether or not we like it. Remember how the Lord stormed Saul's ship one day on the road to Damascus and performed a thorough search without necessarily asking his permission? The result was an eternally changed man—Paul the Apostle—who gave us most of the New Testament! That is why we must give God permission to come aboard. God will work in us *if we let Him.* He will clean us up, forgive us, and take us to heaven *if we'll let Him.*

Lamentations 3:40 says, "Let us search and try our ways, and turn again to the Lord." Let us join God in the search. We must let God search us thoroughly; that means we must sit still, stop squirming, and let Him work. By all means we must let Him clean up what He finds. Just as I challenge friends night after night at our services, we must ask ourselves this question: Why not go one step further and open the door for the Holy Spirit to shine the light in our lives?

## THE SURFACE SEARCH

SEVERAL MONTHS AFTER revival has begun, I received a call from a concerned husband (I'll call him Jim) who was worried about his wife. Her life looked good on the surface, leading a women's Bible study, popular in the church, active in women's ministry. At home she was verbally violent toward him and the children, watched R-rated movies in front of them, and smoked cigarettes. But when she heard the preaching against sin at revival, she grew more and more irritated.

One night, she turned to Jim during the service when I was preaching and said, "This isn't for me. Who does he think he is, talking like he's perfect? He is not talking about *me* that way." Just then, one of our friends who knew her situation at home slipped up to her, asking her if she wanted to go up to the altar for prayer. She took offense, got up, and stormed out of the sanctuary.

She was a good example of the Lord shining a light on her situation: She looked good religiously, but when push came to shove, she did not want deal with this thing called sin. Unfortunately, little sins grow into bigger sins, and this woman did not come back to services. Sadly, she remained trapped in her pride and anger. Only Jesus can give her freedom. First, she must recognize her need for God.

Some of us will not allow God to go any further than the surface of our hearts. Jesus consistently blasted those who limited Him to the surface of their lives. We need to keep in mind that when Jesus walked the streets of Jerusalem, it was common to see freshly painted tombs. This signified to the passers-by the dignity and integrity of the one buried within. Yet Jesus claimed in Matthew 23:27–28, "Woe unto you, scribes and Pharisees, hypocrites! for ye are like unto whited sepulchers, which indeed appear beautiful outward, but are within full of dead man's bones, and of all uncleanness. Even so ye also outwardly appear righteous unto men, but within ye are full of hypocrisy and inequity."

Obviously, the surface search is a joke. These are the people who get up and walk out of revival or church services as soon as the preaching gets a little heavy. These are the lukewarm, laid-back, lazy, unsalty, good-for-nothing Laodiceans John mentions in Revelation 3:16–17: "So then because thou art lukewarm, and neither cold nor hot, I will spew thee out of my mouth. Because thou sayest, I am rich, and increased with goods and have need of nothing; and knowest not that thou are wretched, and miserable, and poor, and blind, and naked." Like so many Americans, we think we have everything but do not even realize our true, sinful condition! We have shrouded ourselves with creature comforts while God is grieving over the true condition of our hearts.

The surface search is worthless because we know how to put on our religious makeup. We adore messages about love, heaven, personal security, and God's provisions. But most of us take offense at the deeper soul-searching words from God. We are accustomed to reaching up and receiving from His hand rather than lifting our eyes and looking upon His face. Yet I believe it is time to seek the *face* of God rather than the *hand* of God! Only then can we expect a great outpouring of His Spirit.

In short, I would rather irritate the daylights out of someone, offend them, make them mad, and sad, and then pray them through to heaven than to stand up preaching a sugar-baby, candy-coated, cream-filled twinkie-type message, watching souls slip right into the eternal fires of hell. Charles Spurgeon once said, "It will be our dull sermons that will haunt us on our dying beds, our tearless preaching, our long studyings, when we might have preached better had we come away and preached without them, our huntings after popularity, instead of saying to the people, 'You are dying, escape for your life and fly to Christ, preaching to them in red hot simple words the wrath to come and the love of Christ."

The surface search: It ain't worth a nickel! Jesus wants to go deeper.

## THE SPOT SEARCH

UNLIKE THE SURFACE SEARCH, this is a little more intense but not much. The spot search means to let God get into selected areas of your life but not all of them. You never relinquish total or absolute control. You allow God to conduct a controlled search, as if you had one hand on the spotlight at all times. In many ways, you are like the rich young ruler in Luke 18:18–23 who asks God for His direction but then goes away saddened by His commands. You let Jesus touch a few areas but when He hits the hot button, you back off, slip out of His presence, and go on your unmerry way:

"And a certain ruler asked him, saying, Good Master, what shall I do to inherit eternal life?" (v. 18). The Steve Hill paraphrase? "Jesus, shine your searchlight right over here for a minute."

"And Jesus said unto him, Why callest thou me good? none is good, save one, that is, God. Thou knowest the commandments, Do not commit adultery, Do not kill, Do not steal, Do not bear false witness, Honour thy father and thy mother." (vv. 19–20). Jesus was turning over rocks. Spot checking. Spot searching. The rich young ruler was doing just fine . . .

"And he said, All these have I kept from my youth up"

(v. 21). And when Jesus heard this, He said to him, "And what's under that rock?" *What rock?* That rock . . . over there.

"Now when Jesus heard these things, he said unto him, Yet lackest thou one thing: sell all that thou hast, and distribute unto the poor, and thou shalt have treasure in heaven: and come, follow me" (v. 22). Oh, that rock. "And when he heard this, he was very sorrowful: for he was very rich" (v. 23). That's the spot check.

Those who only allow God to spot check are the ones who always sidetrack the real issue. Those who only submit to spot searching are those who fidget and squirm, eventually turning their back and walking away when the Lord nails them in the area of their greatest struggle. For example, you might be having a serious problem with anger . . . but instead you let Him deal with your foul mouth. You say, "God, I'm sorry these words slipped out." He is more concerned about the *source* of these words than the words themselves.

One young woman—we'll call her Kelly—told me how God spotted an area in her life through the message one Saturday night in revival. She began to fidget in her seat, growing more and more irritated at the words I was preaching on sin and on the backslidden condition, how there are things that we do that Jesus would never do. Kelly started getting angrier and angrier, until finally she got up and stormed out of the church. She sped through town, pulled up at home, barged into her house, picked up the remote control, and turned on the television.

Kelly was shocked at what she saw: There I was on her screen, still preaching against sin! The next Sunday morning she came to church and gave her life to Christ. She realized that God was performing a search and that she could not get away.

# Searchlights

## A Cellar Search

THE FINAL SEARCH IS WHAT I call the cellar search. This is the search that David the Psalmist was talking about in Psalm 139. This is the search that brings results—total cleansing, eternal fruit, and, of course, revival. This is when you let God clean the "basement" of your soul.

Perhaps you are from the north and were raised with a basement in your home. You know exactly what I'm talking about: There is nothing like a newly cleaned basement. No cobwebs, no spiders, no dark corners. The mid-1800s preacher, Henry Ward Beecher, once said, "No man can go down into the dungeon of his experience and hold the torch of God's Word to all its dark chambers and hidden cavities and slimy recesses and not come up with a shudder and a chill and an earnest cry to God for divine mercy and cleansing."[2]

A cellar search is a complete search. I remember several years ago being at the Madrid airport with a dear friend of mine, Hector Ferreyra. We were travelling through Spain a few months after the tragic explosion of Pan Am's 747 over Lockerbee, Scotland. Upon reviewing our passports, security discovered that I was born in Ankara, Turkey, and that Hector was born in Rosario, Argentina. They felt we could be a security risk and so took us to a back room in the airport.

This back room had two-foot-thick walls and no ceiling. It was constructed for the unintentional detonation of bombs. We were thoroughly searched. In other words, they performed a "cellar" search. Thirty minutes later there was absolutely no doubt that we were clean, so they let us on our flight.

In the same way, Jesus wants to go into the basement of our lives. He wants to go down the creaky, musty stairs of our inner man. He wants to shine the light of the Word in all the cobweb corners of the cellar. He wants to expose those things that have been hidden in darkness. We must let Him discard those things that attract bugs, spiders, and snakes. We must let Him have absolute control because He knows what He's looking for.

This type of humility, this brokenness, this repentance, has laid the foundation for personal and corporate revivals throughout the centuries. It is this same cellar search that has become central to the Father's Day Outpouring.

I like how one journalist described it:

> Churches nationwide are reporting a hunger for God, repentance of sin, renewed interest in evangelism, and a powerful presence of the Holy Spirit in America. These elements and more are found at Brownsville Assembly of God, including,
>
> - Patience . . . a willingness to wait on God
> - Joyful worship; gratitude
> - The name of Jesus is exalted
> - Selflessness; servanthood
> - Respect for the preaching of the Word
> - Orderly church services without quenching the Spirit
> - Passion for God; distaste for stale religion
> - Anticipation . . . an assurance that God will meet them
> - Anonymity . . . an unwillingness to exalt man
> - Acceptance . . . tolerance . . . the understanding that God changes the heart, attitudes, and exterior of new Christians."[3]

These are the fruit of a broken spirit that asks God to

search his heart. And we are continually discovering that these are the fruit of revival. When they are absent, we run the risk of missing an encounter with the living God.

*Chapter Seven*

# Chain of Grace

*One of the two which heard John speak, and followed him,
was Andrew, Simon Peter's brother. He first findeth his own
brother Simon, and saith unto him, We have found the
Messias, which is, being interpreted, the Christ.*

—JOHN 1:40–41

THOUSANDS OF PEOPLE from every corner of the
world have come to our revival services since the
Father's Day Outpouring. Many come not
wanting to miss anything God might have for them.
Consequently, there has been a holy expectancy of the
Lord, a humble submission to letting Him have His way,
to shine His light into hearts, regardless of what the light
may find there.

Young men have been radically set free from addictions;
older women have been healed of lifelong physical ail-
ments; children have captured incredible visions; teenagers

have caught a God-inspired zeal to proclaim Him to their friends; and middle-aged men have been rescued from their "workaholism" to serve the greatest CEO who ever walked the earth, Jesus Christ! The lives of so many precious people have been changed by God Almighty, and a remarkable thing has happened as a result: These new believers have told their friends and brought them to church. The friends, in turn, have gotten saved, and do the same thing with other friends. We have called this glorious move the "Chain of Grace." Each new convert brings another relative or friend to the services, creating a chain-reaction of conversions!

Story after story testifies to the unique and wonderful ways God has reached down from heaven to intervene in the lives of sinners. Each testimony—whether shared in a letter to us or during the revival services—has touched my heart and the hearts of those who hear them. And when reporters from both Christian and secular publications alike come to revival services, as they inevitably have, we encourage them to just listen to the stories of how God has transformed people's lives. Many of these testimonies wound up in print somewhere, documenting the works of God. Who knows the effects these reports are having on the readers?

The Bible says "the testimony of the Lord is sure, making wise the simple" (Ps. 19:7). When we hear the powerful, personal stories of how God has worked in people's lives, our own faith increases, and we are challenged to look to Him even more. Because of that, we regularly hear testimonies during revival services at Pensacola. The following are some of those stories (some in their own words). Each reflects how the Chain of Grace is continuing to build the kingdom. Glory to God!

I have often told others that most people come to

revival for one reason: to get saved. Period. They come because they know someone is going to let them have it. It's like children. You give them parameters and tell them, "This is as far as you can go." And they like it. They are secure in that. Just as they want to know how much Jesus Christ loves them, they also want to know what God requires of them. They get both at the Brownsville Revival.

Sinners know sinners. One or two get saved one night and they blossom into twenty if you give them a few days. Consider the following exciting examples of this "chain of grace phenomenon.

## RADICALLY SAVED

TWO FAMILIES FROM Chicago had been radically changed by the revival and were now actively involved in evangelism. One of the men called me prior to spring break and asked if it would be possible to bring some unsaved teenagers to the revival. My answer was, "Of course! We'll find space for them somehow." A few days later, we were astonished as another call reported that one hundred fifty kids had signed up. By the time they left Chicago, over one hundred seventy piled into seventeen vans and a car and headed to Pensacola.

To shorten an incredible story, one hundred four of these young people were saved in revival. They went back to Chicago and began blazing a trail in the schools. In the corridors of his high school one young man shared with his unsaved friend how he had found Jesus Christ and changed his life. As he spoke, the spirit of God came over him. After he laid hands on him, his friend was hit by the power of God and thrown to the ground. The young man got up twenty minutes later and received Christ as Savior! More lives are being changed everyday, as these on-fire soldiers continue sharing the Good News of the gospel.

Another radical conversion was picked up by the local Pensacola newspaper. Astonishingly the editors gave front-page coverage to the revival, as well as to what Christians had to say about being saved:

> At first, Joseph hated the revival. "I remember not being able to breathe. My head was hurting. I was nauseated. I watched Steve Hill preach, and I hated it." He left, vowing never to return to the five-night-a-week saving sessions at Brownsville Assembly of God.
>
> The next night after work, the twenty-five-year-old Pensacola man went home and discovered everyone was at the revival. "The house was empty, and I was too. I can't explain the emptiness I felt. So I drove to the revival and sat in the back of the church."
>
> He was surrounded by hundreds of worshipers, many seeking the salvation offered by Jesus when He was crucified, then resurrected on Easter. Joseph was looking to be saved from what he described as a life of depression and degradation.
>
> "Steve came up to me, and it felt like he looked right through me. I got freezing cold. I went into a fetal position. Every time he touched me, it hurt, it burned. He began to pray for me. I thought I was flipping out . . . He kept praying for me. Something finally broke and I began to sob from the bottom of my stomach."
>
> The next day, Joseph met Hill for counseling. They talked for hours about the things in his life that were making him unhappy: homosexuality, nudism, the occult, drugs, alcohol. That night, July

10, his parents drove him back to the revival.

"I went to the front row. I told God, 'If you can take all this away . . . the homosexuality, the occult . . . I'll serve you again.' I went to stand, and I fell hard on my face. It was like God was saying, "this is how I want you to serve me."' [1]

God mightily used the testimony from another powerful conversion of a young man named Brian, from Sopchoppy, Florida. He gave his testimony one night during one of the revival services. It was so anointed, the Spirit of the Lord led us immediately into the altar call:

The first book I read as a boy was the Bible. I read it several times, but it never had any power in my life. I went to church off and on, and I even got "saved" once. But I never had any kind of life to show that I was saved. There was no power of God in my life. When I was fifteen I started drinking, and then I got addicted to cocaine, marijuana, all kinds of drugs.

Preachers kept telling me I was saved because I had been baptized and said a prayer one time. But I knew I wasn't right with God. I would do all the stuff that sinners do. How could I be saved? For ten years, I was an alcoholic and drug addict. I went through drug rehab programs, and they couldn't change me. My problem wasn't my environment or circumstances; it was my heart.

I grew angry with God. He never did anything for me. I even blamed Him for taking a girl I loved in a fatal car accident. I got so low that at one point I was with a bunch of friends and our conversation turned to God. Some were saying, "There is no

God." Others were saying, "The earth is our god." I told that them Jesus Christ was God—even though He had never done anything for me.

I was so mad at that moment that I looked up into the stormy sky and said "God, if You are real, why don't You at least use me to show Yourself to all these people? Just strike me dead with lightning right now." No sooner had the words left my mouth than lightning struck a tree just a few yards away. I looked into the heavens again and shouted "You missed!" All my friends began to run in every direction to get away from me. (Incidentally, I wouldn't recommend this type of behavior toward God to anyone now.)

A couple of months later, I spent a Sunday night getting high and drunk, while a local church spent the evening praying for God to save me. The next morning when I went to work, I spoke with an old Pentecostal man who worked with me. He told me that the "fire of God" was on me that day. I didn't know what he meant. All I could feel was a big hollow feeling in my heart. He asked if he could pray for me, so I let him.

When I went to get on my bulldozer in the forest where we were working, my hand suddenly began shaking. I could hardly get the key into the ignition to start the machine. Soon, my whole body was shaking, and I got scared. I fell off of my bulldozer and was paralyzed on the ground. Suddenly, the air changed around me, and I could tell that God was there. I heard a clear voice say to me: "I did not design you to serve Satan. Choose this day whom you will serve. If you don't, I will take my hand off you." I knew right then that I needed to get saved—

for real. When I was finally able, I ran to my Pentecostal coworker and told him what was happening to me. He prayed with me and told me about the revival at Brownsville.

I called a pastor in town and told him that I needed to get saved. He told me to wait a couple of days and come to his church. I didn't have a couple days; I had to get saved now! So I set off for the Brownsville Revival and gave my heart to Jesus.

Since that time, He has given me a new life. I was instantly, completely delivered from cocaine, alcohol, marijuana, and all other drugs. All I can do now is tell people about Jesus. I'm in Bible school because I know that God has a call on my life, and all I want to do is what He wants me to do. Finally His power is in my life, and I know that He can do all that He says He will.

I'm so thankful that Jesus got hold of my life when He did. The Bible says that His Spirit will not always contend with man (Gen. 6:3). He could have given up on me, but He didn't. I know that if I had not obeyed His voice that day in the forest, He would have removed His hand from me forever. Thank God, I made the right choice.

Today, Brian is one of many young people who have relocated to Pensacola to attend our Brownsville Revival School of Ministry. I praise God for their stories. They are just a few examples of the countless ways God has radically saved people at revival. Each proclaims the wonders of God night after night. And there are many more:

- A fourteen-year-old boy was delivered instantly from his eight-year addiction to pornography when a friend invited him to revival services.

- A wealthy, cynical businessman, convinced his wife was in a cult at our revival services, got saved when he came to try to "rescue" her.
- After having seen dramatic changes in her sister who had attended revival services, a former prostitute and drug addict was desperate to find help as she joined her sister one night. She found Jesus!
- A nineteen-year-old honor student realized she could not go on serving two masters and made a conscious decision to get hot for Jesus.
- An eight-year-old girl has been used mightily to intercede for those her heavenly Father is delivering from the pit of hell.
- After seventeen years of alcohol, drugs, failed marriage, and arrests, God began to move in the heart of a forty-year-old construction worker. His teenage daughter came to revival and asked us to pray for her dad; soon he was at church and set free to live a new life for Christ!
- A former nightclub bouncer is now an "on-fire" student in our Brownsville Revival School of Ministry, because he originally thought coming to revival would be a good way to spend time with his father!

The Chain of Grace continues!

## THE FIRE SPREADS

WHAT HAS ALSO CONTINUED to amaze me is that people beyond Pensacola have been powerfully affected by the Father's Day Outpouring. Pastors, friends, workers, Christians from all over the world have come through our doors, experiencing a mighty touch from God and returning home different people from when they came. As a result, the people in their lives have been affected as well.

In powerful long-distance accounts, consider the following ways the holy revival fire has spread:

One man in England wrote,

> Before I became a Christian I was into a very heavy life of organized crime using firearms—actually shooting people. I was charged with murder a couple of times, drugs, burglaries . . . you name it. I spent eleven years in jail. Before I got discharged I gave my life to the Lord. We went through some hard times together, my wife and I. We lived in a car for six months, but I haven't been back in jail since. I'm not going to backslide. I went to my local church (where the pastors had just returned from Brownsville), and God literally pinned me to the floor. I used to be very violent but now that's gone. My temper is gone because God's controlling it.
>
> I go to church every night and Sunday morning. They gave us a car and furniture and actually built our home around us. Now I want to go back to jail, but as a free man. I want to get services started for the convicts. What God forgives is forgotten in His eyes.[2]

A twenty-seven-year-old woman wrote us the following letter:

For years my life as a Christian has been a mask. I confessed that Jesus was Lord of my life, but He did not live in my life. My husband and I were the prime example of lukewarmness. We went to church. I sang Christian music, we prayed to God, and read the Word—but these things were done on our time, when we felt the need to. Yes, I was hungry for more of Jesus, but I did not know which way to turn.

In the middle of February I went home to Ohio to visit family there. Not knowing how my life would be changed, I was in route to a divine appointment. I visited my brother who pastors a small church there. While I was at his home, he talked of the revival in Pensacola, Florida; he and some friends had gone the month before. As they showed me some videos from Brownsville, my hunger for God to move in my life was stronger than ever.

That night we heard that some people from the revival would be at a nearby church teaching on intercession and prayer for revival in our communities. When I arrived, I heard them say that they were there because they were concerned for our souls. My eyes never left them. I wanted God so badly. I had been a dead Baptist girl.

But when the Spirit of God started moving in that church sanctuary, I became fearful. I didn't know if I was ready to lay my whole life down before the Lord, so I prayed, "Lord, if You're going to change me, then change me now. Clean up my heart." Nothing happened. I felt nothing different. People around me began falling out in the Spirit, and I became uncomfortable. I left the sanctuary to visit the restroom, get a drink of water, put on my lipstick—anything to get away from God.

When I finally went back into the church sanctuary, the Spirit of God had fallen all over the place. As I came through the doors, I fell to the floor, completely paralyzed on my back. I was totally aware and not very happy about being on the floor. I said, "God, what are You doing? I feel stupid!" I began to shake. He spoke to me for the first time in my life. He said, "I am changing you. I am cleaning you out." And my life has never been the same since.

That was Saturday night. Sunday night, I fell to the floor and wept uncontrollably for the Baptist church I attended. I saw people from my church (back home) and could not get their faces out of my mind. I pleaded with the Lord to move in their lives. I learned later that the Spirit of the Lord began moving upon the people at that Baptist church. A Spirit-filled missionary was there, and when he gave the altar call, there was no standing room at the front; people were so hungry for God.

Monday night at my brother's home, intercession came over me again, and I wept for my husband who was back in North Carolina where we live. His face was burned in my brain, and I cried out to God to change his life too. I learned later that about the same hour, he returned home from work. The Spirit of God was all through our house. My husband fell to the floor and wept uncontrollably for the sin in his life. God changed my husband right on the floor of our family room. He had no idea what was happening to me in Ohio. God was moving among His people! We didn't actually come to Brownsville Assembly of God until a month later; yet our lives were definitely affected by what the Holy Spirit was doing there!

From Ohio to Ontario, from Montana to Mexico, from New England to New Zealand, from Los Angeles to London, people from all over the world have been touched by God's Spirit, either as they come worship with us in Pensacola or as they visit others who have been here. God's Word does not return void, and it is not limited to the four walls of our little sanctuary!

A ninety-four-year-old Missouri brother wrote us the following letter with his own hand:

> My wife (age ninety-one) and I first heard you from a borrowed VCR on two tapes: "In Wrath Remember Mercy" and "Honey, Where Are We From?" We enjoyed them immensely.
>
> We are very interested in the spread of the saving gospel around the world as we understand you are too. So we are glad to help the harvest, especially overseas. We are two seniors who truly love our Lord!

My heart rejoices at being able to bless and encourage these two dear saints of God.

## PASTORAL CARE

ANOTHER UNIQUE AND EXCITING attribute of this revival has been the many pastors and Christian leaders who have come, many tired from their responsibilities and hungry for a fresh touch from God. Whether it's been at one of our Pastors' Conferences or just attending a service on their own, these humble ministers of the gospel have been refreshed in their own visions. They go back to their congregations with new zeal. And the revival continues.

Before sharing about one such pastor, let me briefly explain the value of a pilgrimage. A pilgrimage is nothing more than a journey, an expedition, or excursion to another place. We all know that hungry Christians have often visited revival centers in order to receive a fresh touch from God. For example, thousands visited 312 Azusa Street to receive from God and take the experience home. Any pastor who says you don't need to go somewhere else to receive from God needs to take his sign down from his church. His sign that reads, "Everyone welcome" is saying, "Come to my church . . . make a pilgrimage." He also needs to remove the ad from the local phone book that reads something like, "Great youth ministry . . . A church for your whole family . . . Come visit us." He's asking people to leave the confines of home, come to his church to receive what they have to offer. Friend, that is a pilgrimage.

The following pastor was one who didn't believe in pilgrimages—but God changed his opinion.

David, forty-six, is pastor of a large church in Arizona. I remember receiving a call from him in which we discussed this present move of God, and why it was necessary for him to come to investigate for himself. David and I had known each other for several years and had developed a trust toward one another's relationship with the Lord. In defending his reasons for not coming, he reminded me that he was "not the type to embrace wild emotionalism." A self-proclaimed conservative in his denomination, he admitted that he had become the "chief of critics," even recently helping to promote an unsuccessful effort to keep a less conservative, well-known evangelist out of his denomination.

Our conversation convinced David that a visit to Brownsville was in order. He overcame his reluctancy and caught the next flight to Pensacola. I had assured him that the Brownsville Revival was not about falling down or shaking, but rather, the primary focus was for souls to be saved and for Christians to receive a fresh touch from God. Dave had never fallen under the power or any such thing. He was considering leaving the service, but decided to stay through the altar call. Afterward, he received prayer. Like so many thousands who come, the Lord met him. He melted to the floor under the mighty hand of God.

Immediately, the Lord became more intimate. David felt in his spirit that the Lord had washed away years of criticism and religion. Concerning his experience he later stated, "All I know is there was such a desire for holiness that I called my wife and told her to cancel the HBO cable channel on our television. My whole atmosphere changed. I was shaking. I had a spirit of intercession," he recalls.

When David returned to preach to his congregation the following Sunday, the power came down! God went to work. Hundreds of people have been running to the altar at David's church ever since. He believes the change occurred when he got out of the way and gave God control. "I am not the same man," David now says. "I laid down my pride. God had to *knock* it out of me."

Another pastor's story is similar. A Pensacola pastor in the Assembly of God denomination, Dan was critical and disillusioned when he learned that revival had come to Brownsville.

"When I walked in there, I said, 'I am not going to fall on the floor.' Three hours later I got up, and the river of God's Spirit has been flowing in me and my church ever since!" Dan has seen over two hundred new converts come to Christ in his church. And he helped spread the Pensacola Outpouring at a series of meetings in another denomination in Arksansas.[3]

One brother, Jim, an African-American pastor in Birmingham, Alabama, started a church in a transitional neighborhood nine years ago with fifteen people. Last year, a white colleague invited this former computer professional to the revival. Jim put it off for as long as he could until finally his friend told him that just as God had called Jim to start the church, now He was calling him to come to a pastor's conference at Brownsville. Though the registration deadline was over, somehow his friend "prayed him in."

Jim reluctantly attended the conference. On one particular night as I called for those who needed forgiveness, Jim started crying. One of our leaders prayed for Jim, and he fell to the ground. When he returned to his church the following Sunday morning, thirty people came to the altar. The next week it was seventy-five, and the next week the whole church came to repentance. Membership at Jim's church jumped from three hundred to eleven hundred within a few months.

"Even white brothers and sisters are coming from other denominations around town. They say this is where revival is breaking out in Birmingham," Jim says. "My heart is for people to know Christ. I don't have an explanation for what is going on. I'm not even sure what to do next. But healings are occurring, drug addicts are getting delivered, and husbands are coming back to their families! We've run out of space . . . all since coming back from Brownsville. Some of my parishioners are thinking of quitting their jobs to go into full-time ministries. This is crazy!"

One Southern Baptist pastor also had to make big adjustments after he attended Brownsville services. He received a "revival anointing," and suddenly God invaded his church in Mississippi. When members of his church planned an evangelistic drama, he was prepared. But even the newly-anointed, veteran pastor was surprised by what happened at those services: twelve hundred people made professions of faith, the drama was extended for three weeks, and white members of his Southern Baptist church had to face their own racist attitudes since the first convert at their services was African-American. Now, other African-Americans from the small Southern town are visiting this church for the first time ever. The Holy Spirit is at work rooting out sin, refreshing the hearts of the saints, and bringing new sheep into the fold all the time. Many congregants are trembling and shaking in repentance during the services.

"People in my church have been held back by tradition, but they are ready to bust loose!" the pastor says.[4]

John, a pastor from the Northern Territory of Australia, reluctantly came to the revival . . . he wasn't sure he should be away from his ministry for a few weeks. But God touched his life while he worshiped with us, and when he returned home, he saw God work in ways he hadn't seen before. A friend told him he had been a "dead man" before he went to revival: now he seemed "resurrected."

John had a burning desire to see souls saved, and so he began to pray with members of his church for their small town. Crime, sexually transmitted diseases, and alcoholism were rampant in their area. He went on a ten-day fast, played Pensacola tapes every night at home and at their ministry center, and prayed specifically for the local leaders.

Not long after that, the mayor's wife came by John's ministry, a drop-in shelter for local homeless men. She asked him simply to tell her about his work there. Then she wanted to know "about God." For three hours, John shared the Good News of Jesus Christ with this elite woman, a woman who had never been to this part of town. She asked if she could come to his church and bring other friends, the very people John had been praying for! "God is doing something real good at home. Even my wife, who's only seen the Pensacola videos, has been changed by God's power because of the revival!"

## "GO BACK"

YES, FRIEND, LEADERS FROM Methodist, Amish, Mennonite, Presbyterian, Baptist, Pentecostal, Episcopalian, and a host of other churches from around the world have taken revival back to their sanctuaries and congregations. Entire communities are being affected by this great outpouring of God as a result. Families are reuniting, prodigals are coming home, and the lost are being found by the love of God.

Young and old alike from a variety of backgrounds, in Pensacola and beyond, are being touched by the Spirit of the Holy God in life-changing ways. Why? Because they are encountering the Living Person of Jesus Christ, not some old religion or tradition!

This incredible Chain of Grace reminds me of the passage in Matthew 11:1–6 where Jesus instructs John's disciples to go back and tell him what they have seen and heard:

> And it came to pass, when Jesus had made an end of commanding his twelve disciples, he departed thence to teach and to preach in their cities. Now when John had heard in the prison the works of Christ, he sent two of his disciples, and said unto

him, Art thou he that should come, or do we look for another? Jesus answered and said unto them, Go and shew John again those things which ye do hear and see: The blind receive their sight, and the lame walk, the lepers are cleansed, and the deaf hear, the dead are raised up, and the poor have the gospel preached to them. And blessed is he, whosoever shall not be offended in me.

The blind are receiving their sight, the poor have the gospel preached to them. It is true: Jesus, the Son of God, our Messiah and Savior, has come to us! And we cannot quit testifying to what we have seen and heard!

*Chapter Eight*

# Words From the Waters

*Then they that gladly received his word were baptized; and the same day there were added unto them about three thousand souls.*

—Acts 2:41

GOD KNOWS OUR PAST as well as our future. Eighteen years ago, He saw me start out on a road that was going to destroy me, and He tried to warn me. As teenagers, we used to get together in someone's car and go "cruisin" on Friday nights. One particular night we had done that. We weren't old enough to buy alcohol, so we needed someone else to buy it for us. I approached a man I thought for sure would do it. He was in an old broken-down pick-up truck, he wore dirty clothes, and his hair was messed up. He looked like he would buy us some alcohol.

"'No,' he said, 'but I've got something that will get you higher than alcohol.' Of course, we all thought he meant drugs. He reached in his back pocket and pulled out a picture of Jesus Christ. That shook me up. But it didn't change me.

"I kept on going down the road, and sure enough, eighteen years later, it about destroyed my life. At first I wanted to drink. It was fun and social. It went from there to me hating drinking. I couldn't stand it, but I couldn't stop. It was destroying my family, and they hated it. Six months ago, about a week before I started coming to the revival, I was at work at a restaurant. I was cleaning a table when I noticed a man seated at a table in the corner and witnessing to someone. I heard this man say how Jesus had taken away his desire for alcohol, and how He had taken away the cussing, anger, and hatred he had in his life.

"So standing there in the middle of that restaurant, wiping the table, I said, 'Jesus, I am so tired, and I can't do it by myself. Just take it. I don't want it anymore. Just take it!' My prayer lasted a few seconds. I went home like I always did and reached for a bottle of wine. But I didn't want it and put it back in the refrigerator. The next day I didn't want it. Weeks went by, and I still didn't want it. In fact, it has been six months, and I have not had one withdrawal, not one desire for alcohol. People tell you that alcoholics never recover. Well, this one is not recovered. I am not reformed. I am redeemed and delivered by Jesus Christ!"

This is just one example of the hundreds of testimonies we have heard each Friday night during our baptismal services at Brownsville. As I listened to this woman's story on this particular night, I sat with tears pouring from my eyes . . . I knew from my own experience what she was talking about! It was incredible to watch what happened next: As the leaders got ready to baptize her, she bowed in half and trembled so much from God's Spirit that they could hardly baptize her! Coming up from the water, she literally had to be lifted out of the pool because the power and blessing of God were so strong on her!

That is what happens when the Chain of Grace continues—brand-new Christians are washed clean through this simple act of obedience. Each Friday night, we celebrate how God has taken a sinner and made him or her a saint in His eyes. We hear their public confessions of faith, and we see before our own eyes the transformation that comes as a result of water baptism. And those of us in the family of God are blessed because we have heard the powerful reminders of His wonders; we have come to call them "words from the waters."

## LIFESAVERS

WHEN SOMEONE IS DROWNING, we don't yell at them from the dock to get out of their predicament. We don't simply watch and say, "Gee, it's too bad you're drowning. Wish I could help." Of course not. We offer the drowning man more than encouragement; we give him what we *know* will save him! When we see someone struggling in the deep, we quickly throw him a life preserver, a raft, or a rope to keep him from dying. Or we just reach in and pull him to safety ourselves.

During baptism, a person is dunked in death, so to speak, and comes up in the new life of Jesus Christ. It is the Holy Spirit of God who pulls him out of the deep darkness and into the light of life. He is saved by the great life preserver of the Word made flesh! And these new believers respond with a glorious zeal to tell others of their salvation experience.

You can imagine what a joy it is to hear the countless stories of how God pulled these drowning victims out of their predicaments and offered them living waters instead! So powerful are their baptismal testimonies, that I had to share a few of them.

## SHE COULD NOT STOP TALKING . . .

ONE YOUNG GIRL was saved and delivered from years of pain, guilt, and unforgiveness as a result of sexual abuse. Soon her parents came to know the Lord as well. Why? Because she "could not stop talking about what she had seen and heard." Consider her story:

"I am seventeen years old and live in Florida, not far from Brownsville. I grew up going to Sunday school at a Methodist church, but I didn't know the Lord until about one-and-a-half years ago. I was always the 'good older sister,' always behaving, always making good grades, always nice. I had everything I wanted.

"But I was miserable inside. I had a wonderful family, but I wasn't communicating with them because I was lost, confused, and hurt. I was holding back a terrible secret. When I was a child, I had been sexually abused by my dad's younger brother. He was living with us while he went to college. My parents had no idea. For years I had to deal with him coming over to the house and pretending. One time I was deliberately rude to him. My mom noticed and yelled at me, but I couldn't give her the real reason for my actions. I had to try to block it out. *It will be all right if you just forget,* I told myself. And I almost did.

"I remember the night it all came back to me. I watched a documentary movie late one night about a girl in my exact situation. It hit me: *This was me. I was in the movie.* I cried myself to sleep.

"It started haunting me again. Every time I turned around, I saw 'sexual abuse . . . get help . . . tell someone . . .' Tell someone? I could hardly say the words. But I knew eventually I would have to tell someone. I knew it would tear up my parents, and I was scared that they wouldn't believe me. I thought once I got it out, things would be okay. I was wrong.

"Things went crazy. My parents were hurt and angry for me. My grandparents didn't believe it. At first my uncle denied it, and I was forced to go to counseling to talk about it. I actually had to explain in detail what he had done! It was torture. I pushed the whole episode to the back of my mind. Life went on, though miserably.

"Then the Lord got hold of me. I got a relationship with Jesus. At least I thought I was fine for about a year. Until I came to Brownsville. During the altar call one Friday night, I clawed, I sweated, my heart pounded. I prayed, 'Lord, what is this? I thought everything was fine!' 'No, get up!' He said. I sat some more, clawed some more, pounded some more.

"Finally, I came down to the altar and cried like a baby. I knew what I had to do. I had to forgive. I fought it, but I kept seeing Jesus on that cross forgiving me, forgiving me, forgiving me.

"That was the night I got saved. I was set free and delivered. My life was changed. I went home the only Christian in my family. I started praying and praying for my family. Not long after that, my brother got saved, and two weeks later, my parents came to Brownsville and gave their lives to the Lord.

"Then I knew I wanted to be baptized. God was laying on my heart to share about what I'd been delivered from. I fought it again. But He kept saying, 'Yes . . . yes.' When I stepped into that pool, I knew I had to say it. And I did. Jesus stood next to me and held my hand! Just months before I couldn't even say the words 'sexual abuse,' but by the grace of God I could share my secret with thousands of people at the revival. I was set free! And I realized there were people out there looking at me saying, 'That's me! I need to do what she's doing.' Now I'm a totally new person—no hate, no bitterness, no anger—all because of the blood of Jesus. I forgave!"

This young woman has been coming with her family to revival services ever since her baptism celebration.

## WILLIAM

THAT YOUNG WOMAN experienced the saving hand of the Lord, as did William, whose "words from the waters" show how he literally was able to help save another soul:

"I am William, and a week ago I was saved. The Monday before that, I sat at work as an agnostic, a borderline atheist. I didn't know where I was going, or what I was doing. A friend started telling me about the Lord, but I just wanted to sit and work and not pay attention to him. The more he talked, though, the more I had to listen Finally, I didn't have any more work, so I listened more intently to what he said. He just didn't stop talking about Jesus, and eventually he invited me to Brownsville.

"I went and accepted Christ. Now I know God is with me and leading me. Not long after that, I even felt as if I should stop by a little church one day. I had passed it many times before but never stopped. On this one day, I attended a service there when a little boy started choking in the pew in front of me. His mother and grandmother started to panic when he gagged. They didn't know what to do. But I did . . . I gave that little boy the Heimlich maneuver, and out of his mouth shot a peppermint candy. Right then, I knew why I had to go to that church that day!"

## NEW LIVES, CLEAN HEARTS

NOT ONLY HAVE SOME NEW converts helped throw "life preservers" to others, but many who have experienced radical transformations have been able to invite others to the same cleansing waters of God's love. The following stories are living proof of what happens to others when a soul is rescued from dark and troubling circumstances:

One young man had spent some time at Brownsville Assembly of God Church many years ago as a youth. When his family moved to another state, he stopped pursuing God and ran from Him for seven years. A friend invited him to revival and, as he says, the Lord "got hold of my heart. He set me free from an addiction to gambling. As a child I was stealing all the time, and I never thought I could break that addiction. I used to go into grocery stores, stealing this and eating that and not paying for either. Then right after I got born again and God touched my life, I went into the grocery store with a friend. I picked something up and he asked if I was going to steal it. I said, 'No, the Lord's touched my life now.' I know now He's got hold of me for good. Hallelujah!"

One woman from Pennsylvania had frequently visited a crack house in her neighborhood. She grew desperate for each hit, but realized she could not take it much longer. She called her aunt who she knew was a Christian and asked her to come and get her. She did.

This young woman's aunt and uncle then decided to show her videos from the Brownsville Revival. But before her uncle could get the videotape in the VCR, he was slain in the Spirit for forty-five minutes! His niece decided then and there to get to the revival somehow. When she came, she soaked up everything she could. She came to the altar and received prayer. Before being baptized, she told the congregation, "For sixteen years I have been in and out of drug rehabilitation programs. I have tried to commit suicide three or four times. In fact, last year I ate eighty Valium, and my heartbeat was less than six beats a minute. I was almost dead.

"But praise the Lord, I'm here. Last Friday night, I was prayed for. I had smoked almost two packs of cigarettes a day for more than six years. Saturday morning I woke up and crushed five packs of cigarettes and have not wanted one since. God has done so much every day, every day. I am so excited. Next week I am leaving for Teen Challenge. Whatever God wants to do, I am going to let Him do it. He who has begun a good work in me is faithful to complete it!"

Another woman also took hold of God's hand as He pulled her from a life of drugs:

"I spent most my life searching for . . . Jesus. I was searching for His love and His sweet Spirit. But I just couldn't find it. About five years ago, I thought I was coming to the end of my search. I lost hope, and I didn't want to live. I lost my mind and ended up in a mental hospital. For years I was on about five different kinds of medicine. I would save it up, you know, just for when I couldn't handle it anymore; the torment in my mind, the pain in my heart were great. Sometimes I would overdose on the most powerful pills. I'd cut and bite myself. But God's arm wasn't too short to get me.

"All my life I was rejected. My father forsook me. But here God told me, 'I am your Father!' Can a mother forget the child she bore? 'Even though she may forget you . . . I will not forget you!' I know the love of Jesus now!"

Gary, a sweet brother, also knows that saving grace:

"I came to revival for the first time a month-and-a-half ago. I came here as a pot-head, smoking at least three joints every day. The first thing I was told was that I was brought here by divine appointment. The second thing was that they had spent hours in prayer that God would 'prepare the heart for the message and the message for the heart.' Then they brought two pot-heads to the platform who told how God delivered them from their addiction.

"That night, I realized God is real, and He would do a work in my life. I came forward and prayed. I said, 'God, I want what those people have, the work You did in their lives.' He answered my prayers, and I've been free from addiction! No struggling with it. I've been totally freed, and now I don't even think about it. Thank You, Lord Jesus!"

One West Virginia man told us that God had delivered him from a twenty-eight-year alcohol problem when he gave his heart to the Lord at the revival. He had been drinking three half-gallons of rum each week and many beers. When he quit drinking, he didn't get sick, and he didn't miss alcohol. "The Lord just took it away from me. I gave my heart to the Lord then. Tonight in baptism, I'm going to give Him the rest of me. I'm going to serve Him the rest of my days!"

## OUT OF THE WATER

THESE WONDERFUL BAPTISM testimonies keep going. One woman was saved from a ten-year lifestyle of homosexuality and drugs; another man who had manufactured cocaine and sold it was thankful God "reached down" and took him; another was delivered from seven years of obsessive-compulsive disorders; and one college student on spring break at home watched his mother's Brownsville videos, came to revival, and exchanged his life of partying for new life with Christ.

Each testimony reflects not only a new sense of purpose but a deep desire to do what God requires. Yes, the hearts of these new believers have been changed, but their lifestyles are also radically transformed. For many, an intense burden for the lost is born in them during these times, and consequently, they begin to share their new saving faith every chance they get.

Consider Jill who, with tears of joy rolling down her cheeks, quietly but confidently proclaimed before she was baptized, "He's healed my heart. I was molested when I was a child. I hated men. I wanted to go to hell just to torture every child molester. Now, all I want to do is take as many to heaven with me as I can!"

One big, middle-aged man was shaking and shouting as he told us, "I'll never be the same! I was so empty, and I kept trying to fill it with all kinds of things. Alcohol, sex, pornography. But the Lord touched and delivered me here. Listen, devil, your kingdom's going to fall. It's going to fall! I've got the Lord Jesus!"

Jeff had been in the military. He never imagined he would be in front of the Brownsville congregation, testifying of God's mercy as he stood in waist-high water: "About three years ago, I got in a relationship with a woman that I never have should been involved in. The Lord tried to sway me another way, but I was too set on my own ways. I got in a car wreck, and it damaged the front part of my brain pretty badly. The doctor said it would be damaged for life.

"I got so depressed, I overdosed on sixty elavil and sixty

inderal, and, if you know about medicine, you know that dosage will kill you. Flat out kill you. I fell asleep in some remote part of the hospital and by some odd happening, my commanding officer showed up. I was a scary sight, but he got me to the emergency room, and now, I am here today. I am alive. The odd thing about it is now I counsel suicidal people. A couple of years ago, I would have told everybody that I don't need to be saved. I am not worthy of being saved. But God has shown me another way. I just want to go with Him!" When Jeff emerged from the pool, he threw up his hands in triumph!

One woman from Brooklyn, New York, also shared a triumphant story as she stood in the water: "The Lord brought me here from Brooklyn. I have a young daughter that I am believing to be delivered from drugs. I have my grandson here who is five, a granddaughter who is three, and one who is three months old. They are all withdrawing from crack and heroin. I asked permission to raise them, but I found myself not just griping and complaining in my heart, but yelling. I kept saying, 'Cleanse me, Lord, make me clean.' Not only for my babies, but for all the babies out there and the parents who are still doing drugs. I felt that the good I was doing I was somehow undoing because I hadn't let the Lord change my heart. So I repented of trying to do it myself and getting caught up in the works of the house instead of seeking Him. I was trying to please other people, losing time to seek Him.

"And so I lost my relationship with Him. But tonight I want to proclaim that I want it back. I want to know Him more and serve Him more. I want to be used for these children. Not just mine but all children. I want to be used for the prostitutes and the drug addicts in the streets. I want to go to New York to be used by God, not just for my daughter, but all the daughters and sons out there. The ones in the offices, where their parents think that since they've been through college, they are fine. But they aren't fine! They are drug-eaten. They are lost. I ask that when I go back I will be so changed that no one will know me. That the love of Jesus will flow through me so that when I'm squeezed, only the love of Jesus will come out! I ask to be changed, my God."

## FINAL WORDS

WHEN AN INDIVIDUAL ENCOUNTERS the living God, like Paul did on the road to Damascus, he or she is changed in no small way. And the lives of those around him are affected as well, especially by the cleansing of sin that comes through baptism.

From personal experience, I know what happens when a soul meets the Maker of the Universe. Everything changes. That individual's commitment is all the more solidified when he is washed in water, coming up into God's presence. Jesus commanded believers to be baptized for that very reason. And the words from those cleansing waters cannot cease anymore than the mighty river of God can:

- "I would like everyone who knows Jesus to intercede for me because I need a real move of God. I did not come here just to get wet tonight, but I want God to totally ratify my life."
- "He delivered me from drugs, alcohol, nicotine, and a homosexual lifestyle. Praise God! Now I am pressing in daily, believing for my deliverance from AIDS. Tonight I am believing to be delivered completely of anything that could be left. Publicly, this had to

be taken care of in Jesus' Name."

- "I lived seven years in Satanism, and it is nothing compared to what I have experienced coming here to revival. I just want to praise God for what He has done in my life these last two days."

- "I am so thankful for this revival. I was a completely different person before. I was raised in a Christian home, but I never knew God. I do now, and He is my best friend. I am in love with Jesus and vow to Him tonight that I will never leave Him."

- "I want to thank the Lord for His mercy and His grace. To those of you who are not saved yet, you feel like you don't want to give up your sins. God has been faithful in taking things away from me that would bring me back to the world. He has been that way in several areas of my life. You don't need to worry about what you need to give up. Just let God have it."

- "Wednesday night my husband bring me to church. I from Thailand. I don't believe God. My daughter pray for me twenty-two years, my other daughter pray twenty-five years. They say, 'Mom, go church.' But I got temple. I say no. They say, 'He touch me all the time.' They say, 'I want you go with me church.' I come Wednesday. I walk in the door. I close my eyes. I feel God. I know God now. I love God, and I do anything for my Jesus. I leave and go home. I throw away my stuff, my Buddha. Buddha never do anything for me. No more Buddha, no more Buddha!"

- "I came here two weeks ago, in anger, to watch my former homosexual lover get baptized. He left me because of his new relationship with Jesus. I sat through the service. The Holy Spirit convicted me of my sin, and now I'm saved! I'm here tonight, obeying God in His command to be baptized."

- "I got away from God because I wanted to fit in at school and be accepted by my friends. But now, I don't care what they think. I'm going after God!"

- "All I can say is I finally know peace. I lived with guilt for many, many years and I finally know peace."

- "I am in the United States Navy. I am on my way to Sicily, and I wanted to be baptized before I left. The only thing that comes to my mind is Acts 1:8 where it says, 'But ye shall receive power, after that the Holy Ghost is come upon you: and ye shall be witnesses unto me both in Jerusalem, and in all Judea, and in Samaria, and unto the uttermost part of the earth.' That is what I plan to do for the next two years in the Mediterranean."

Yes, to the uttermost parts of the earth, God's holy river is flowing. And our world needs His great outpouring now more than ever before! We cannot afford to miss His mighty cleansing touch. Our lives, and the lives of those around us, depend on it!

## Chapter Nine

# How to Miss God

*. . . because thou knewst not the time of thy visitation.*

—LUKE 19:44

A S I WRITE THIS, IT IS ALMOST two years since that Father's Day when God first poured out His Spirit on us. Revival has continued five nights a week since then, and over one hundred thousand individuals have made commitments to follow Jesus Christ. Many have been baptized. Others have received a fresh touch from God and testified of His amazing grace and intervention in their lives. It has been an amazing and exciting process for me to be involved in.

Yet it has not been easy. The Christian life seldom is, especially when we live in a world so full of spiritual tensions. I will never forget one night after revival services when a man ran up to me in the Brownsville sanctuary. Panic was in his eyes, and urgency shook his bones. He had come to the revival the night before, but in the middle of the service he decided he'd had enough. He told me how he got up and left the church to go drinking.

His decision led him to a local pool hall where he drank a few beers, laughed, and shot pool with some friends. While involved in the game, he suddenly fell under conviction that he should be back at the church listening to the Word of God. He tried to shake it off, but the conviction was too hard to bear. He said good-bye to his friends and entered the sanctuary just as I was giving the altar call. Then this middle-aged man did a remarkable thing: He literally ran down the aisle to me and accepted Christ as his Savior.

With stammering lips, he recounted how he later found out that one of the friends he had been drinking with was involved in a fatal car accident. Shortly after he left the pool hall, his friend also left, but did not join him at church. Instead, his friend engaged in a high-speed race through downtown Pensacola in his Corvette. Driving at over one hundred miles per hour, his car flipped over, killing him instantly, and scattering debris from the Corvette over two blocks. This man, obviously shaken, told me, "I would have been in that car. I would have missed God."

## ENTERING THE FIGHT

MANY PEOPLE FIND THEMSELVES in similar situations of missing God, not fully understanding the spiritual implications. But we must remember that this is war; we are all involved in a life-and-death battle. The battleground is the mind, and the spoil of war is the soul of man. Paul said it well in Ephesians 6:12, "For we wrestle not against flesh and blood, but against principalities, against powers, against the rulers of the darkness of this world, against spiritual wickedness in high places."

There is a battle raging in the heavenlies over every living soul on earth. Satan and his demon forces know if they can distract a man from going after God like the man in the pool hall, or if they can deceive a person by giving him just enough truth to satisfy him, it will prevent him from entering into a vital, day-to-day relationship with the Lord Jesus.

Let's think for a minute how easy it is to miss God. The Scriptures relate the stories of two individuals who received from God. Both are instructive in telling us how they received from God, even though they could have easily missed Him. I believe the following stories are especially crucial for those working in the ministry who could easily miss a mighty heaven-sent revival; yet they are also for those who have never met the Lord and are wavering in the valley of indecision.

If we could hear personally from the characters in these two stories, I'm sure we would hear them declare the mighty works of God. I like listening to people who have received from God. But I have to be honest: I am fed up, as I am sure you are, with folks who could talk all day until they're blue in the face from vomiting opinions. Opinions are like garbage cans: everyone's got one and most of them stink! They talk all day about God, but don't really know Him. They ridicule everything God is doing in other men's ministries while glorifying their own. You get the blues from listening. They talk, talk, talk, and all the time they haven't really said anything.

I want to hear someone who has received a legitimate

life-changing miracle of God. That is why the following two examples are so powerful. Found in the Gospel of Mark, the first is the story of the woman with the issue of blood (5:25–34); the second is the healing of blind Bartimeus (10:46–52). From these two stories we can glean four essential points on how we can easily miss God:

1. Don't listen to the Word of God.
2. Listen to everyone else's opinion.
3. Trust your own understanding.
4. Do absolutely nothing when Jesus passes by.

## CLOSE YOUR EARS

> "And a certain woman, which had an issue of blood twelve years, and had suffered many things of many physicians, and had spent all that she had, and was nothing bettered, but rather grew worse, when she had heard of Jesus, came in the press behind, and touched his garment. For she said, If I may touch but his clothes, I shall be whole. And straightway the fountain of her blood was dried up; and she felt in her body that she was healed of that plague" (5:25–29).

The beginning of the woman's miracle came when she opened up her heart to hear about Jesus the healer. In other words, she had ears to hear. The Bible says, "When she had heard of Jesus. . . ." She was moved to respond, to take action about her sickness. Someone came to her and told her about Jesus. She had the choice to shut that person out, or to open up and listen. She decided to listen.

In the same way, revival encourages people to listen. All types come to Jesus for a fresh touch. And because I am an evangelist, I have to take this opportunity now: If you are reading this and have not yet come to the saving knowledge of Jesus Christ, you also have a choice to make. You can decide to harden your heart and not permit the seed of God's Word to take root. Or you can choose to be open and pliable, allowing God to work in you that which pleases Him. Perhaps you are a minister and have not yet opened up to receive a fresh touch from God; it is your choice as well to reach out to Him and allow the time of refreshing and healing to come!

Remember, if you do not want a miracle in your life, don't you dare listen to God's Word! Don't listen to the preacher! Why? Because the Word of God will prick your heart, arouse you from your spiritual slumber, get you on your feet, and out the door. The Word of God will shine a light on your sin, expose it, root it out, and nail it to the cross. "For the word of God is quick, and powerful, and sharper than any twoedged sword, piercing even to the dividing asunder of soul and spirit, and of the joints and marrow, and is a discerner of the thoughts and intents of the heart" (Heb. 4:12). Yes, like the woman in the story, God's Word gets inside of us and changes us!

However, if anyone wants to miss God, he should not listen to the Word of God. He should not listen when the preacher says, "Come to Jesus and He will heal you, come to Jesus and He will save you. No one loves you like Jesus; He's the only one who can set you free."

The woman with the issue of blood had everything else distracting her, but she was unyielding in her resolve to get a touch from God.

If we want to miss God, we need to start getting distracted and do anything we can to deter our attention from the message. In our study time, we should get distracted by turning on the television set, flipping through the radio, putting down the book, or shooting some hoops. Anything but letting God's sword pierce us.

Many people who are satisfied with status-quo Christianity will not pursue God. But the Christians in the New Testament and those throughout church history were not status-quo Christians—they pursued God with all their hearts. It's all or nothing; either we listen to God or we miss Him.

## GARBAGE OPINIONS

> And they came to Jericho: and as he went out of Jericho with his disciples and a great number of people, blind Bartimeus, the son of Timeus, sat by the highway side begging. And when he heard that it was Jesus of Nazareth, he began to cry out, and say, Jesus, thou son of David, have mercy on me . . . And Jesus stood still, and commanded him to be called. And they call the blind man, saying unto him, Be of good comfort, rise; he calleth thee. And he, casting away his garment, rose, and came to Jesus. And Jesus answered and said unto him, What wilt thou that I should do unto thee? The blind man said unto him, Lord, that I might receive my sight. And Jesus said unto him, Go thy way; thy faith hath made thee whole. And immediately he received his sight, and followed Jesus in the way (10:46–47, 49–52).

The second step to missing God is to listen to everyone else's opinion. Bartimeus is a good example of this. According to the Word of God, he received an incredible healing, but he had to fight the hellish, critical crowd to get it. The crowd around Bartimeus told him to be quiet;

they didn't think Jesus would do anything for him. "Many charged him that he should hold his peace" (v. 48). In basic vernacular, they were telling this loud, obnoxious blind guy to shut up.

It's a good thing Bartimeus did not listen to the opinions of others. Likewise, I believe it's time we learn that the majority does not rule. When it comes to Christianity, narrow is the way that leads to eternal life, and few find it. Just because the crowd is saying one thing does not mean they have the answer. The majority opinion does not translate into truth. And in the case of the particular situation of Bartimeus, the crowd was dead wrong; they were more blind than he was. He was surrounded by religious zealots who had their physical eyes wide open while their spiritual eyes were sealed shut. These people were stuck in the mud of religious activity and would never experience revival as long as they stayed there. As Leonard Ravenhill once said to me, "Religion is hanging *around* the cross. . . . Christianity is hanging *on* the cross."

Night after night in the revival services there are hundreds of people who experience a radical change in their lives. Many of these people have been what I would call nominal Christians. They received Christ as Savior at one time in their lives but are not committed to Him in their everyday life. He has been their Savior, but He is not their Lord; He is not currently governing their lives.

Yet they sit under the preaching of the Word at revival and realize their spiritual deficiency. Often with tears in their eyes, they come to the altar in repentance. The change in them is so radical that many other "religious folks" take offense and make statements such as, "You don't have to be so holy. Jesus never intended us to live that perfect. Why do you have to go to church all the time? You're not any better than I am! You don't have to read your Bible so much." These are honest statements that we hear all the time at revival, critical statements that flow from lukewarm hearts.

I am reminded of Sandi, a young lady who gave her heart to the Lord at the revival not long ago. Having recently graduated from high school, she spent the weekend on a wild drinking spree in New Orleans. When she returned from her weekend on the town, Sandi ran into Brooke, an old high-school friend whose life had been radically changed by God because she attended the revival services. Sandi at once grew jealous and desirous of the same peace and joy her friend now exuded. Brooke invited Sandi to the revival, where she, too, was wondrously saved.

Sandi had never been to church in her life and did not own a Bible. She, like her mother, always believed that basically everyone would go to heaven, that a "good God" wouldn't send anyone to hell, and that one can worship whatever they wish. When Sandi returned home, her mother, still of this basically New Age belief, became worried about the changes she saw in her daughter. Soon she restricted Sandi from coming back to the revival. Her mother told her she'd rather see her drunk than see her become a "religious fanatic."

"It's not necessary to be so emotional about God, to waste your life away in church. You are no longer permitted to attend," Sandi's mother said. How this young woman responded to her mother was a true sign that Jesus had touched her life: Sandi submitted to her mother and stayed home for two weeks. Sandi continued to love her mother. She did not argue with her; she even prayed God would change her mother's heart. But slowly she fell into a depression. Though her motives were right, she had listened to someone else's opinion and allowed it to affect her life negatively. As an eighteen-year-old, she was independent enough to make her own choices.

She went to her mother again, expressing her desire to go to church. Sandi's mother said she would think about it. The next morning, Sandi remembered the Scripture that said she somehow had authority over the devil. She was at a breaking point when she jumped on her bed and yelled to the devil, "Get your hands off my family! I'm not going to take it anymore!" She rebuked the devil from her house, saying, "I'm a new Christian, I'm growing as a Christian, and *I'm going to the revival.*" We wrestle not with flesh and blood!

That afternoon, her mother brought a package into her room and told Sandi she had a gift for her. In the box was an expensive, leather-bound Bible recently purchased at the local gospel bookstore. "Sandi, I'm proud of you and what's happened in your life. I give you permission to go to the revival." If she had listened to her mother's earlier admonitions to avoid becoming a "religious fanatic," she would have gone back to her old ways. But she was patient and God eventually changed the situation.

My point is, Sandi got around negative opinions and let herself listen. For two weeks, she listened to lies instead of truth, and went into a spiral of depression. Like the woman and like blind Bartimeus, Sandi was told it would never happen. Yet Jesus passed by her way and touched the situation!

Like Sandi, many others at our revival services almost missed God because they listened to the opinions of others. Today, Sandi and her friend, Brooke, are students at the Brownsville School of Ministry. Remember, there will always be a wave of opposition against us when we begin to enter the deeper things of God. If we desire revival in our churches or in our personal lives, we must get ready to face the persecution.

## TRUST YOURSELF

WE CAN MISS GOD BY letting other things distract us or by listening to the opinions of others. But we can also miss Him by trusting in ourselves.

Of these two stories in the Book of Mark, I believe the woman with the issue of blood could best enlighten us on the danger of trusting in our own understanding. Certainly, her own understanding said, "All hope is lost." According to the Word of God, she had been sick for twelve years, had spent all her money, had seen all the doctors, and yet had grown steadily worse. And besides, there was a huge crowd around Jesus; people must have told this woman that she would never get through to Him.

This certainly sounds like a hopeless situation. I can imagine her thinking, *You've always been like this and you always will be like this. So get used to it.* She could have trusted in herself for healing but instead she pursued God—in spite of herself and her seemingly hopeless situation!

Our natural minds cannot understand the things of the Spirit (1 Cor. 2:14); therefore, our minds will try to find an escape route. In other words, our natural minds will say, "God will never forgive you for all the bad things you've done!" Our natural minds will major on how bad the circumstances are rather than on how great God is. Our natural minds will say our family will never receive Christ; they've always been drunkards, they've always avoided God, they've always watched Christianity only from a distance. Our natural minds will say, "Revival will never come to this church. These people don't want revival. I will never see miracles, signs, and wonders within these four walls."

Our own understanding has an ally. The natural mind

has a best friend, and his name is Lucifer. Our own under-standing coupled with the lies of Lucifer will bring certain spiritual death. Yet the Bible says in Proverbs 3:5–6, "Trust in the Lord with all thine heart; and lean not on thine own understanding. In all thy ways acknowledge him, and he shall direct thy paths."

In other words, things are not always as they seem to our natural minds. For instance, a few months ago my nine-year-old son, Ryan, and I were out together for a drive. He said something that I really didn't pay much attention to at the time. As we passed by a condominium construction site where a huge crane towered above the structure in progress, Ryan looked up at the crane and said, "Daddy, would that thing ever fall over?" My imme-diate response, without even considering his desire for a more detailed answer, was, "No. It would never fall over because the man operating it knows what he's doing." Ryan accepted that answer, and we continued on our way.

Two hours later we were heading back by the same site, only to find the road in front of the site barricaded by police. A police officer said there would be a four-hour delay in passing. Why? A construction crane had fallen over onto the highway! It had fallen on a car, from which a woman and her daughter barely escaped death. That was the very spot where Ryan said to me, "Daddy, would that thing ever fall over?" It was the same crane!

That incident reminded me of how we so often believe that "everything is certain." We go along firmly set in our own understanding, our own way of thinking, convinced that everything is okay. It all just works out. And our only foundation for this belief is "because it's always been that way."

This is dangerous. Too often we put our trust in things that are very untrustworthy. I have learned over the years to put my trust in the Lord. The Bible says, "Trust in the Lord with all thine heart . . . " Of course, my own understanding is, "Yeah, those cranes never fall down because man knows what he's doing. He's building those things." That is how people are with Christianity. They say, "Yeah, yeah, yeah. I've got enough of this mainline Christianity."

But man *is* fallible! Sadly, some of us have leaned on our own understanding concerning a great move of God in our lives. We believe God is going to do things in a certain way. Or we see God as "the way He's always been in our lives," and we just can't imagine anything else. That is our own understanding.

It's time to recognize that God's ways are not our ways. His thoughts are not our thoughts. He can do anything He wants, anytime He wants. He is not limited to our reasoning ability. He is not limited to our mentality or intellect. He can go far beyond it. He can raise the dead. He can heal the sick. He can open the blind eyes. He can deliver us from our financial oppression. He can set us free from the bondages that have been plaguing us all of our lives. God can do it! Our own understanding says He can't free us, but God says He can. Our own understanding will tell us that God won't forgive us, when the Word of God says He will wash away our sins.

In short, when we trust in our own understanding instead of God's boundless ability, we miss the powerful blessings of God.

## JUST DON'T DO IT

THE LAST STEP IN HOW to miss God is a classic: do absolutely nothing. When Jesus passes by, just sit there. Blind Bartimeus can testify to the difference between just sitting there or going after God. He would never have received a miracle if he had chosen to keep his mouth shut and his feet planted and just sit there, allowing his opportunity to pass him by.

The opportunity of a lifetime must be seized during the lifetime of an opportunity. When we hear about Jesus, when we hear that He can heal us, when we understand that God is near, we can, of course, just sit there. We can do absolutely nothing. We can refuse to go after God, refuse to cry out, refuse to do a thing, and I guarantee—God *will* pass us by.

However, I am determined *not* to miss God. I am convinced that we are at the beginning of one of the greatest awakenings this country has ever known. That's why I have determined in my heart to be a part of what God is doing.

The other day I imagined myself sitting on a couch twenty-five years from now with a grandchild on my knee. He looks me in the eye, and says, "Granddad, what was it like back in the nineties? What was it like during that great revival? Where were you when millions of Americans gave their lives to Christ?"

I turn to my grandchild and say, "I was right in the middle of it. I did everything I could to be a part of that mighty move of God."

Don't be the one who hangs his head in shame and mumbles to his grandson, "I missed God, son. I didn't think all that commotion back in the nineties was God. But as it turns out, I was wrong."

Yes, it's up to each of us—pastor, lay leader, Christian—to determine in our hearts not to miss God. Each of us must turn our hearts to Him for revival and make up our minds that we will be one of those who did all we could not to miss God. And so, instead of missing God, we must seek Him with all our hearts. That means being honest with ourselves right where we are—right now.

## SEEING GOD, SEEING OURSELVES

MAN SEES PEOPLE IN SOCIAL and emotional contexts, but God looks at the heart. Throughout the Word, we find four types of people:

1. *People who are close to the truth*—such as the Ethiopian eunuch found in Acts 8; those who are trying to find God but have not yet tasted of His goodness or turned their lives over to Him.
2. *People who are distant from the truth*—such as the Samaritan woman in John 4 who was living in sin and was astonished at the revelation of Jesus Christ.
3. *People who have known the truth but have backslidden*—such as the prodigal in Luke 15; who had experienced the joys of living with his father, rebelled, and found himself hopelessly lost and in need of restoration.
4. *People who know the truth, have been set free, and live in victory*—like the apostle Paul.

All four types have the ability to miss God. But the truth of Jesus Christ and the power of the Holy Spirit can turn anyone in His direction once a person sets his heart toward Him.

## Chapter Ten

# Bring Revival
# or We Die!

*Call unto me, and I will answer thee, and shew thee great
and mighty things, which thou knowest not.*

—JEREMIAH 33:3

WE *NEED* REVIVAL. We do not want to miss
God's great outpouring because each of us,
from the youngest to the eldest . . . our entire
country . . . is in desperate need of a spiritual awakening, a
mighty move of the All Powerful Lord. Just as Jesus Christ
called me out of a life of drugs and evil and sent me
around the world to proclaim His name, so, too, is He
calling each of us to come out of darkness and into His
marvelous light. We need God to move in our lives, and in
our land, over and over again. He is our only hope.

The following is a report of a recent event that should

bring hope to every man, woman, and child in America. The event took place in Montgomery, the state capitol of Alabama. Read this report by Douglas Hawks, and rejoice with us over what God is doing in America:

> We've all seen the typical political rally: the band . . . the placards . . . the red, white, and blue streamers. We've heard the rehearsed rhetoric and seen the slick smiles of polished politicians: campaigning, mud-slinging, fund-raising. Rallies are a dime a dozen in this politically-charged, issues-oriented society.
>
> But, friend, I have never beheld anything like what took place on the State Capitol steps of Montgomery, Alabama, on April 12, 1997! Oh yes, the band was there . . . singing "Our God is an Awesome God." The placards were in place . . . displaying the Ten Commandments. And the twenty-five thousand who gathered that day got more than the usual double-talk and hoopla. The message that day was simple: personal and national repentance and holiness in the sight of Almighty God.
>
> The "Save the Commandments Rally" was arranged as the battle continued after a federal court ordered Etowah County Judge Roy Moore to remove the plaque displaying the Ten Commandments from his Alabama courtroom wall. Judge Moore, however, refused to remove the Word of God which this nation's government was founded upon from his courtroom. Alabama Governor Fob James, Jr., firmly supported Judge Moore's stand, willing to enlist the defense of the national guard, if necessary.

140

The rally in Montgomery had a two-fold purpose. First, it was organized to offer support to Governor James and Judge Moore, two men who love God and are soldiers in His army. Secondly, to proclaim the truth of Jesus Christ and the need for repentance and revival across the United States of America.

For the first time in decades I was truly proud that I was an American. For years, like so many others, I have been disgusted and ashamed of the filth and sin that America so often represents. I remember ministering in the former Soviet Union. They made no secret of their anger toward us as Americans, since their nation that had been infested with American drugs, American pornography, and America's own MTV. The shame of a country whose leaders have been involved in trying to cover up their crimes . . . all the while outwardly professing faith in God. Watergate, Iran-gate, Whitewater— proud to be an American?

But friend, that Saturday in April, as the Pledge of Allegiance was given under an overcast sky, rays of hope began to break through just as the sun was breaking through the clouds overhead. As I listened to the messages delivered by Governor James, Judge Moore, Alabama Attorney General Bill Pryor, and Dr. Alan Keyes, I realized that these men were not here to speak about a "generic god," but to lift up the name of Jesus Christ. They didn't back down, bow out, or shy away from the real issue at hand: God the Father, the Son, and the Holy Spirit as the only hope for our country. National pride began to rise up in me. *America can still fulfill its God-given purpose.* Under the leadership of men like those I heard speak from the steps of the Governor's Mansion, we can be a strong nation, under God, again.

The Brownsville Revival Ministry Team had been invited to speak at the rally. Pastor Kilpatrick, true to his first call as a pastor, stayed home, as he had been scheduled to perform a wedding for two of his members that day. Several from Brownsville made the four-hour trek to the state capital to be in supportive and prayerful attendance. Michael Brown and Stephen Hill were given over thirty minutes to close the meeting. Rally organizers were adamant about the conclusion being similar to a Brownsville Revival meeting. One organizer, Pat Mahoney, turned to Mike and Steve and said, "We want this to be a repentance rally. Let God use you . . . say what's on your heart!"

When the officials announced that the rally would "now be turned over to the leadership of the Brownsville Revival," I expected news crews and attendants to begin packing up and heading out. However, such a cheer went up from the crowd when they announced who was going to close, no one left. With twenty-five major and regional news stations recording, and four hundred radio stations tuning in, a clarion call to repentance went out that would be in the ears of America from coast to coast.

People had been excited, rowdy, and cheering on the speakers all day. But now it was time for a decision, a call to change. The message was clear: "Many of you have a deep concern over the possibility of the Ten Commandments being removed from the court house wall, yet you removed them from the walls of your heart long ago. Others of you have

142

stood in the hot sun rallying around God's people, singing Christian choruses. . . . But in just a few hours, you will be at home screaming at your family and guzzling a six-pack of beer! America is sick of the hypocrisy! Mainstream America says they 'believe' in God, 'believe' in Jesus, 'believe' they will stand before God and be punished for their sin! But of those 80 percent, nearly 100 percent still live in rebellion and sin. If there is sin in your life and you are calling yourself a Christian, *change your name!* You are a heathen—at best a backslider. There is hope! Jesus Christ loves you and has a plan for your life. He died on a cross two thousand years ago to give you new life. Now it's up to you to do something about it."

Steve Hill said to me, "America is ready for revival. It is time. I have never been so convinced of this as when I stood before this massive sea of humanity and made this call to repentance." Without hesitation, without any secrecy . . . no eyes closed . . . thousands upon thousands of hands shot into the air confessing a need for forgiveness and a desire for repentance. As Charity James sang "Mercy Seat," dignitaries seated to my left and right with lifted hands dropped to their knees, weeping in repentance. In the crowd, everyone from Bikers for Jesus to pro-life activists, flag-waving Confederates to camera-toting newscasters, dropped to the pavement under the convicting power of the Holy Spirit. As far as the eye could see, people were getting right with God. There were tears of repentance, there were prayers of repentance, there were hearts broken over sin and made right with God. As Governor James described it later: "We had revival on Dexter Avenue!"

Indeed, it is the same message that has been preached for almost two years in what is known as the Brownsville Revival.

## THE HANDWRITING ON THE WALL

IT HAS BECOME OBVIOUS to me that this revival is turning into the greatest awakening America has ever seen. If we stop now, we will be the biggest disgrace of heaven and the laughingstock of hell. At this point there can be no retreat, no stopping. God is going to send an awakening to America that will, in the end, shake the whole world. I believe this meeting in Montgomery was a shadow of things to come in this nation. I can see the handwriting on the wall. I will not be surprised when the message of repentance and holiness is preached from the steps of this nation's capitol and the Ten Commandments are displayed and obeyed in every courtroom, classroom, and government edifice from Washington, D.C., to Washington state. D. L. Moody said it well: "If God be your partner, make your plans large."

Those in attendance at the Brownsville revival meetings will often hear me shout: "Do it again, Lord!" Perhaps I am referring to His healing miracles of the past, "Do it again!" Or maybe to His mighty outpourings of years gone by, "Do it again, Lord!" After all, if Jesus is the same yesterday, today, and forever (Heb. 13:8), then why can't He perform His same mighty acts in these modern times? I am convinced that He, and He alone, is mighty to save.

## MEMORIAL STONES

IF YOU HAVE READ THIS FAR, you must also want to experience God in new and powerful ways. You and I are both burdened for revival for our country, and throughout the world. But how? We must, of course, be prayerful, humble, and hopeful that God will move. And, I believe, we also must look back in order to move ahead.

Remember how Joshua commanded the Israelites to preserve several memorial stones from the Jordan River as reminders for God's miraculous intervention? I, too, have personally found that, in addition to God's Word, reading historic accounts of revivals also often fuels my fervor for more of God. From the pages of history, I am reminded of, and encouraged by, God's gracious and incredible wonders He performed in and through His people.

In his book, *The Revival We Need,* Oswald J. Smith whets our appetite for more of the Lord:

> It was in 1904. All Wales was aflame. The nation had drifted far from God. The spiritual conditions were low indeed. Church attendance was poor. And sin abounded on every side. Suddenly, like an unexpected tornado, the Spirit of God swept over the land. The churches were crowded so that multitudes were unable to get in.
>
> Meetings lasted from ten in the morning until twelve at night. Three definite services were held each day. Evan Roberts was the human instrument, but there was very little preaching. Singing, testimony, and prayer were the chief features. There were no hymn books; they had learnt the hymns in childhood. No choir, for everybody sang. No collection; and no advertising.
>
> Nothing had ever come over Wales with such far-reaching results. Infidels were converted, drunkards, thieves, and gamblers saved; and thousands reclaimed to respectability. Confessions of awful sins

were heard on every side. Old debts were paid. The theatre had to leave for want of patronage. Mules in the coal mines refused to work, being unused to kindness. In five weeks twenty thousand joined the churches.

In the year 1835 Titus Coan landed on the shore belt of Hawaii. On his first tour multitudes flocked to hear him. They thronged him so that he had scarcely time to eat. Once he preached three times before he had a chance to take breakfast. He felt that God was strangely at work.

In 1837 the slumbering fires broke out. Nearly the whole population became an audience. He was ministering to fifteen thousand people. Unable to reach them, they came to him, and settled down to a two years camp meeting. There was not an hour day or night when an audience of from two thousand to six thousand would not rally to the signal of the bell. There was trembling, weeping, sobbing, and loud crying for mercy, sometimes too loud for the preacher to be heard; and in hundreds of cases his hearers fell in a swoon. Some would cry out, 'The two-edged sword is cutting me to pieces.' The wicked scoffer who came to make sport dropped like a dog, and cried, 'God has struck me!' Once while preaching in the open field to two thousand people, a man cried out, 'What must I do to be saved?' and prayed the publican's prayer, and the entire congregation took up the cry for mercy. For half an hour Mr. Coan could get no chance to speak, but had to stand still and see God work.

Quarrels were made up, drunkards reclaimed, adulterers converted, and murderers revealed and pardoned. Thieves returned stolen property. And sins of a lifetime were renounced. In one year 5,244 joined the church. There were 1,705 baptized on one Sunday. And 2,400 sat down at the Lord's table, once sinners of the darkest type, now saints of God. And when Mr. Coan left he had himself received and baptized 11,960 persons.

In the little town of Adams across the line, in the year 1821, a young lawyer made his way to a secluded spot in the woods to pray. God met him there and he was wondrously converted, and soon after filled with the Holy Spirit. That man was Charles G. Finney.

The people heard about it, became deeply interested, and as though by common consent, gathered into the meeting house in the evening. Mr. Finney was present. The Spirit of God came on them in mighty, convicting power, and a revival started. It then spread to the surrounding country until finally nearly the whole of the Eastern States was held in the grip of a mighty awakening. Whenever Mr. Finney preached, the Spirit was poured out. Frequently God went before him so that when he arrived at the place he found the people already crying out for mercy.

Sometimes the conviction of sin was so great and caused such fearful wails of anguish that he had to stop preaching until it subsided. Ministers and church members were converted. Sinners were reclaimed by the thousands. And for years the mighty work of grace went on. Men had never witnessed the like in their lives before.[1]

Someone recently read Smith's book and said to me, "That sounds like the Brownsville Revival!" Yes, friend, *this* is the revival we need! Again I pray, "Do it again, Lord! Have mercy, Lord! Wake us up from our shameless slumber."

To which God has replied, "Tell them, Steve, that I will pour out My Spirit once again. I will again show mercy. I will bless My people. I am stirring My church. I am coming back for a glorious church without spot or wrinkle."

## THE PURIFYING PROCESS

A TRUTH I HAVE LEARNED through the revival at Brownsville is that people want to be stirred. They want to be blessed and washed so that they will be "without spot or wrinkle." I have learned that America and the world are ready for what I call, "True Christianity." Why do I believe this? From all over the earth, almost 1.5 million people have slipped into this sanctuary (or anywhere else on the premises they can find to stand or sit). They are not coming to see a show or to hear an eloquent preacher. If they were, on both points they would leave extremely dissatisfied.

As the evangelist, I try always to practice what William Gurnall, a conservative minister of the 1600s pointed out, "He that thinks to please men goes about an endless and needless work. A wise physician seeks to cure, not please, his patient." I do not approach the pulpit or the page to please or impress anyone, either with my oratory skills or eloquence of words, for in these I am deficient. I do, however, approach either those in the congregation or those reading this book as a dying man speaking to dying men. I share as a man who was created from dust, and to dust will return. I come as a human being who has tasted of the poisoned fruit of sin and suffered the consequences. I have personally experienced the destructive powers of the devil.

However, I am thrilled to report that Jesus Christ came two thousand years ago to destroy the works of the devil and to give us an opportunity to live life in abundance today! I have personally experienced the redeeming power of the Lord, which qualifies me to come to you with good news—very good news! No matter where you have been or what you have done, there is forgiveness in Jesus Christ.

That forgiveness is attained through humble repentance and reaching forth to be washed by the blood of Jesus, individually as a child of God, and corporately as a nation. America was founded by men who depended upon God Almighty as the supreme power and magistrate, first in their personal lives, and thus through its government. Personal repentance and corporate reliance on the Maker was the purifying process that laid a foundation for our land. The same must be true today.

## HUMBLE PROCLAMATIONS

EVIDENCE OF THESE BELIEFS is laced throughout the declarations of our nation's government, though we heed them not. Abraham Lincoln is one of our most powerful examples. Lincoln, the sixteenth president of the United States, came to the point of personal repentance and faith in Jesus Christ while in office. His faith had a profound effect on the future course of our government and nation.

The following proclamation recorded on March 30, 1863, heralds Lincoln's recognition of the need for the nation as a whole to come to the same humble repentance that had gained him mercy and pardon from his own sins. Hear the words of "The Proclamation Appointing a National Fast Day":

Whereas, the Senate of the United States devoutly recognizing the supreme authority and just government of Almighty God in all the affairs of men and of nations, has, by a resolution, requested the president to designate and set apart a day for national prayer and humiliation:

And whereas, it is the duty of nations as well as of men to own their dependence upon the overruling power of God, to confess their sins and transgressions in humble sorrow yet with assured hope that genuine repentance will lead to mercy and pardon, and to recognize the sublime truth, announced in the Holy Scriptures and proven by all history: that those nations only are blessed whose God is the Lord:

And, insomuch as we know that, by His divine law, nations like individuals are subjected to punishments and chastisement in this world, may we not justly fear that the awful calamity of civil war, which now desolates the land may be but a punishment inflicted upon us for our presumptuous sins to the needful end of our national reformation as a whole people?

We have been the recipients of the choicest bounties of heaven. We have been preserved these many years in peace and prosperity. We have grown in numbers, wealth, and power as no other nation has ever grown.

But we have forgotten God. We have forgotten the gracious hand which preserved us in peace, and multiplied and enriched and strengthened us; and we have vainly imagined, in the deceitfulness of our hearts, that all these blessings were produced by some superior wisdom and virtue of our own.

Intoxicated with unbroken success, we have become too self-sufficient to feel the necessity of redeeming and preserving grace, too proud to pray to the God that made us!

It behooves us then to humble ourselves before the offended Power, to confess our national sins and pray for clemency and forgiveness.

Now, therefore, in compliance with the request and fully concurring in the view of the Senate, I do, by this my proclamation, designated and set apart Thursday, the 30th day of April, 1863, as a day of national humiliation, fasting, and prayer.

And I do hereby request all the people to abstain on that day from their ordinary secular pursuits, and to unite, at their several places of public worship and their respective homes, in keeping the day holy to the Lord and devoted to the humble discharge of the religious duties proper to that solemn occasion.

All this being done, in sincerity and truth, let us then rest humbly in the hope authorized by the Divine teachings, that the united cry of the nation will be heard on high and answered with blessing no less than the pardon of our national sins and the restoration of our now divided and suffering country to its former happy condition of unity and peace.

In witness whereof, I have hereunto set my hand and caused the seal of the United States to by affixed.[2]

Think of the incredible circumstances which surrounded Lincoln's amazing document! When the senate approached the president in 1863, our country was divided by the horrific deception of pride and hatred which had erupted into the Civil War. Brother was killing brother in the streets. Sons turned against their fathers, daughters against their mothers. Bigotry and hatred spewed into death and mayhem. A nation which Lincoln once recognized as having grown in numbers, wealth, and power as none other, had "vainly imagined, in the deceitfulness of [their] hearts, that all [the] blessings were produced by some superior wisdom and virtue of [their] own." It was a deception that destroyed countless homes and families.

This tragic lesson from our past beckons us to consider America today. We have been lulled to sleep by the intoxication of success and the apparent lack of divine punishment for our sinful lifestyles. The words of Solomon are hauntingly true: "Because sentence against an evil work is not executed speedily, therefore the heart of the sons of men is fully set in them to do evil" (Eccles. 8:11). In layman's terms, because God has not come down in judgment and wrath, we feel everything is okay. What a lie. How can we remain unmoved as nightmares fill our newscasts? America rarely rolls over anymore as reports of gang massacres, mass suicides, militant-armed cults, racial beatings, rapes, murder, and mayhem are sensationalized in the news and later become box-office hits! Then we parade around bestowing honor after honor on each other as if all the gains and advances which this country has enjoyed were "produced by some superior wisdom and virtue of our own."

Why doesn't America now hear an alarming cry for revival from her governmental guardians? Because there is none. Religion, like an incompetent nanny, is gently pulling the covers up over America's head and tucking us comfortably in at Satan's slumber party. It is indeed a wicked bed of unrest in which this nation dozes. Oh, yes,

America will wake up. But, will it be like a frightened child awakened by a nightmare, only to find it is eternally trapped in the inescapable horror of hell? Or . . . let us pray . . . will America awaken to the opportunity for genuine repentance, which is the only thing that brings true peace and rest?

If one of my own children screamed out in terror in the middle of the night, what kind of father would I be if I ignored him, letting him scream and cry and continue to be tormented by a nightmare because he couldn't wake up? Should I just go pull the covers over his little sweating, trembling body, tuck him in tight, and without a word, return to my bed? No, of course not. I would run into his room as fast as I could, pull him up in my arms, and firmly say, "Wake up! Wake up, Honey, you're having a bad dream!"

If that is the response of an earthly father, what do you think will be the response of our Heavenly Father to those of us living the nightmare of our country's present reality? Remember, He loved us so much that He gave His only begotten Son, that whoever believes in Him should not perish, but have eternal life (John 3:16). Surely, He will awaken our nation to His truth and mercy once again.

## DAYS OF DECEPTION

LINCOLN WAS UNDER REQUEST by the government and by the decree of God to make the Proclamation in 1863, and to awaken the nation with a loud cry for genuine repentance. In a similar way, I believe I am also under a strict mandate from the Lord. I believe His order to me was direct:

Preach what I have placed upon your heart. Do not

hesitate. Do not put it off. Remember, Steve, you will not face man on Judgment Day; you will face Me. You will be held accountable for every word and deed. I am doing a deep cleansing work. Speak, my son, to the darkness. There must be Light for Me to continue My work. Many are cloaked in the darkness of sin. Just as I spoke to the darkness and the Light overcame it, so speak to sin and My Spirit will overcome it. I will forgive today. I will heal their backsliding. I will deliver those in bondage. I will create life where there is death. This is a new day.

We must examine ourselves as to what sort of "spiritual sleepers" we might be. Perhaps, hopefully, you are one who wakes easily, one who by hearing the Word of God cry from these pages, will be brought to a point of decision and, I believe, will make the right choice. You are someone who will receive the Word of God, allow the Holy Spirit to plant the precious seed deep down in the soil of your heart, and respond by bringing forth the fruit of repentance. In just a few short minutes, you will get right with God and spend the remainder of your days with joy unspeakable coupled with a peace that passes all understanding.

But what if you are a more sound sleeper? One who will hear the Word and unwittingly allow the hardness of your heart to bring you comfort as you drowsily say: "Yes, Preacher, that's the truth. I need to make things right with Jesus. I need to allow the Holy Spirit to convict me of sin and permit the blood of Jesus to cleanse me from all unrighteousness. I need to quit hanging around the cross and get on the cross. I need to shake myself from my spiritual slumber and get serious about the things of God. But not right now. Let me sleep a little longer; perhaps I'll hear you tomorrow concerning these things." Be careful! Like Peter the night he denied Christ, though you are standing close to Jesus, by your actions you deny you even know Him!

And, of course, you may be one of those spiritual "scripture scrooges" who receives the Word as the clear, untainted, pure message from God and then blurts out, "Leave me alone! That's a bunch of hogwash. God never expects us to live like that. You can't be serious, Preacher! Surely, you're joking." You are the one who will turn away, mock, laugh, attempt to vomit out your disgust on companions and friends, and then step from the light back into your miserable life of darkness.

To you, I loudly proclaim: "Friend, it is totally up to you!" Night after night I see the people God has drawn by His Spirit to the meetings to wake them up. Yet, one can be weeping while the other is mocking. One can be melted like wax while the other remains cold as ice. One can cry while the other curses. One can be convicted under the mighty hand of God, while another, sitting right next to him, sits daydreaming about the next sin, filled with all forms of wickedness. One can be embraced in the arms of the Lord while the one right next to him is slow dancing cheek-to-cheek with the devil.

All these responses are recorded in the Bible. Paul the Apostle experienced these three kinds of people upon the conclusion of his powerful message to the crowd in Athens on Mars Hill, "Some began to sneer, but others said, 'We shall hear you again concerning this' . . . But some men joined him and believed" (Acts 17:32–34, NAS).

With intense scrutiny, we must consider the challenge not to be lulled to sleep by religion! By definition, *religion* is "a faithful, ardent adherence to a system of beliefs." That means a fisherman is religious. Serious golfers and compulsive Monday night football fans are religious about their sports. A computer technician is religious about his work.

I want to warn every reader about what is taking place in this nation. The subject of God is becoming popular. We must beware of the upcoming religious rage. A *rage* means "a *fad*—what's fashionable, the in thing, the latest trend, in vogue, popular." The Bible warns us that in the last days people will adhere to a *form* of religion but deny its *power* (2 Tim. 3:5). We must be careful because this form of Christianity is becoming popular, not unlike the commercial fads that have taken our nation by storm: hula-hoops, slinkies, tie-died tee-shirts, wide ties, narrow ties, neon-polyester clothing, sushi bars, nose rings, body piercing, Internet chat rooms, mood rings, platform shoes, belly chains, saggy pants and plastic clothes. Now we are entering a season of spiritual seduction complete with all its toys and alluring trinkets: "Holy hula-hoops," "spiritual slinkies," "Tickle-me teachings."

A religious rage is upon us. It has become faddish to talk about God. Consider the weekly secular magazine racks which testify to this with their posh covers; they've presented every shape and form of angels, questions about heaven, mysteries of prayer, and quandaries about the meaning of life after death. God has become just another character on prime-time television, angels are in full force in major motion pictures, and religious jewelry and clothing are right in style. Yes, God is becoming marketable. Of course, God has *always* sold, but now people are selling Him—and that is quite a different thing.

## ON THE HORIZON

I SEE IT AS AN APPROACHING cloud on the horizon. As

Charles Spurgeon said, "The form of godliness always involves attendance to the ordinances of Christianity, attendance with the assembly of God's people and religious talk." Why? Because of the respect it will bring the participants. . . . it's the in thing! But beware, you can talk about heaven and still go to hell. You can know all about Jesus and still not know Jesus. You can go to hell with a choir robe on. You can be the founding member of the largest church in town and one day find yourself in hell. You can go to hell with a certificate of ordination from the Assemblies of God, the Southern Baptists, or any other denomination, hanging behind your desk. The walls of your home can be adorned with plaques and certificates giving notice to your past religious contributions while your heavenly bank account stands in bankruptcy.

I like how William Gurnall, a preacher in the 1600s, stated it: "The sweet bait of Christianity hath drawn many to nibble at it who are offended with the hard services it calls to. It requires another spirit than the world can give or receive to follow Christ fully." We will see more and more advertisements and programs that are willing and ready to market this newfound public craving for spiritual things. It is a religious rage and will sweep through our society like the wind. It is being fueled today by popular public opinion. Things will look spiritual, smell good, feel right. People will talk right, walk right, sit right, but something won't *be* right!

We must beware! We can be lured into a lukewarm religious philosophy that will damn our souls. Paul warned us to avoid these people in 1 Timothy 3:5. Their teachings and beliefs are like hidden reefs in the sea. A perfect example of this is found in the country of Barbados, where there stands a monument to the truth of deception. The story is that during the 1800s, Sam Lord's castle was used to lure unsuspecting ships to their doom. Being a pirate, it was Sam Lord's method of operation to go about hanging bright lanterns in the trees of his dark estate. Seeing the light of the lanterns and believing them to be the lights of safe harbor, beguiled captains would steer their ships toward the castle. The truth of deception was suddenly exposed as the jagged reef, which protruded from the ocean floor around the castle, violently ripping open the hulls of the ships. Sam Lord, seeing his prey like a fish caught in a net, would swiftly row out and plunder the ships of his hapless victims.[3]

Today, I see lanterns in the trees! We cannot afford to be lured in by all the commotion about God and Christ, or succumb to any religious fad. We must remember the true definition of Christianity, the true call of Christ. To be a Christian means to be Christ-like. That is, like Christ! True Christianity is signified by a separation from the world of sin in which we live. It refers to going after God, pursuing holiness, being sanctified, forgiven, a believer (adherer) in Jesus. It is to be, as the Bible says, a child of God, child of Light, salt of the earth, servant of God, soldier, witness, vessel of honor. It is to have brought death to the old self by being made a new creation in Christ, displaying the fruit of the Spirit: love, joy, peace, patience, kindness, goodness, faithfulness, gentleness, self-control (Gal. 5:22). To be a Christian, we must first be on the cross. There are no detours. No easy outs. No catnaps. No alternatives.

We can sit under the greatest preachers in the world, own the most extensive biblical research library in the nation, confound the End-Time teachers with our prophetic knowledge, soak up the teachings of the most celebrated educators of our day, saturate ourselves with biblical cassettes and videos. We can subscribe to magazines like *Christianity Today, Charisma, New Man, Decision,* and others, faithfully listen to *Focus on the Family,* permit our children to watch only Christian videos and read Christian books, have the largest Christian music CD collection, know backward and forward the seven steps to church growth, the five easy lessons to maintain a successful Christian life, and the three surefire methods for a believer to rid himself of bad habits.

We can do all the important Christian deeds, but if we have not been redeemed, if we have not been to the cross, if His blood has not washed away our sins, then we are as lost as a junkie on the streets! (And I know what that's like!) Each of us must listen to *and* adhere to the four spiritual laws:

1. All have sinned (Rom. 3:23).
2. Sin separates us from God (Rom. 6:23).
3. God has provided a remedy for sin's penalty (Rom. 5:8).
4. This remedy must be applied personally and received (Rom. 10:9–10, 13).

If anyone fails to adhere to these steps, he is doomed to a life without God. He might be holding to a form of godliness, but he is denying the power of God to work in his life, especially if he hasn't dealt with sin. Almost two thousand years ago, the anointed pen of Paul sketched out the truth of what we are seeing today. In 2 Timothy 3:1–7 he warned:

> But realize this, that in the last days difficult times will come. For men will be lovers of self, lovers of money, boastful, arrogant, revilers, disobedient to parents, ungrateful, unholy, unloving, irreconcilable,

malicious gossips, without self-control, brutal, haters of good, treacherous, reckless, conceited, lovers of pleasure rather than lovers of God; holding to a form of godliness, although they have denied its power; and avoid such men as these. For among them are those who enter into households and captivate weak women weighed down with sins, led on by various impulses, always learning and never able to come to the knowledge of the truth (NAS).

## The Necessity of Revival

PAUL MIGHT AS WELL have been describing our country in the 1990s! The sad statistics prove it and the evidence to prove that we need a national revival:

- When 80 percent of adult Americans, expecting to be called before God on Judgment Day to answer for their sin, are still sinning . . . We need revival![4]
- When nearly one million Americans are populating federal and state prisons . . . We need revival![5]
- When there is a 5 percent rise of reported murders annually . . . We need revival![6]
- When 77 percent of Americans believe they are going to heaven and only 6 percent believe they are going to hell . . . We need revival![7]
- When American teenagers commit more than four thousand homicides a year . . . We need revival![8]
- When the number of juveniles arrested for serious crimes is rising to 130,000 a year, a

55 percent increase over the decade before . . . We need revival![9]

- When 95 percent of American teenagers say they believe in God but don't live like it . . . We need revival![10]

- When we have one minister for every seven hundred Americans (compared to one for 115,000 people outside the United States) and so little change . . . We need revival![11]

- When major denominations are allowing practicing homosexuals to be ordained . . . We need revival!

- When Americans are burning up the psychic hotlines . . . We need revival!

- When college newspapers are printing opinions such as, "I think [Jesus] hangs out at band parties. And he probably even has an extra lighter ready in case anyone needs one. I think he greets people inside the door [of the bar] with a handshake" . . . We need revival![12]

- When there are literally thousands of "millennia-madness" cults . . . We need revival!

- When groups like Heavens Gate and the Branch Davidians and militant racist organizations are constantly increasing . . . We need revival!

- When America allows more than four thousand unborn babies to be murdered daily, yet it claims to want more of God on television . . . We need revival!

- When music projects like Marilyn Manson's "Antichrist Superstar" reach the top of record sales charts . . . We need revival!

- When suicide is the third leading cause of death among fifteen-to-twenty-four-year olds . . . We need revival![13]
- When heroin is being used by more than 1.4 million people across America . . . We need revival![14]
- When Americans spend an average of seven hours and forty-two minutes a day watching television . . . We need revival![15]
- When 63 percent of American teenagers say they go to movies and "make out" on dates . . . We need revival![16]
- When 64 percent of Americans believe that all marriages will end in divorce . . . We need revival![17]
- When there are some 917,410 sexually explicit pictures, pornographic descriptions, short stories, and film clips on the Internet . . . We need revival![18]
- When there is a demand for images of perverse sex acts on the Internet that cannot be found in the average magazine rack . . . We need revival![19]

Send revival, dear God, or we will die!

## "HEAR OUR PRAYER"

THE SPIRIT OF THE LORD is sweeping through the land. He is visiting Pensacola, Florida, and He continues to breath forth His holy fire throughout the nations. I can hear the cry of the concerned Shepherd to His slumbering sheep: "Awake America!"

Yes, we need revival. And thank God, He is going to

"do it again!" He has already begun. He is hearing our prayers; He is among us and more than willing to satisfy the hungry heart that has been awakened to holiness.

My prayer for each of you reading this book is that you do not let this present move of God pass you by. Determine in your heart to receive everything the Lord has to offer. Do not settle for the status-quo religion, old religion, or stale tradition. Jesus Christ is ready to forgive you and transform you from darkness into His saving light!

Arise, oh people, and seek your God. Determine in your heart to be in constant pursuit of revival!

# Notes

## CHAPTER ONE:
## THE GREAT CALAMITY

1. Noah Webster, *The American Dictionary of the English Language*, 1849, s.v. "obligation."

## CHAPTER SIX:
## SEARCHLIGHTS

1. John Flavel, *A Treatise on Keeping the Heart* (New York: American Tract Society, 1835), 33–34.
2. Henry Ward Beecher, Life Thoughts, . . . Discourses of Henry Ward Beecher (n.p. 1858), 25.
3. Hal Donaldson, "Mr. Bush in Pensacola . . . Editor's Journey," *Pentecostal Evangel*, 10 November 1996, 5.

## CHAPTER SEVEN:
## CHAIN OF GRACE

1. Alice Crann, "Troubled soul finds salvation during Brownsville revival," *Pensacola News Journal*, 7 April 1996, 1.
2. Daina Doucet, "Pensacola: 25,000 Saved," *Spread the Fire*, August 1996, 8.
3. Lee Grady, "Suddenly, God Came," *Charisma & Christian Life*, June 1996, 49.
4. Ibid.

## CHAPTER TEN:
## SEND REVIVAL OR WE DIE!

1. Oswald, J. Smith, *The Revival We Need* (New York: Christian Alliance Publishing, n.d.), 11–13.
2. William J. Federer, "The Proclamation Appointing a National Fast Day," *America's God and Country, Encyclopedia of Quotations* (Coppell, Texas: FAME Publishing, Inc., 1996), 383–384.
3. "Sam Lord's Castle," *Barbados, Just Beyond Your Imagination* (Hansib Caribbean: St. John's Antigua, West Indies, 1996), 135.
4. George Gallup, Jr., "Religion in America . . . 1996" (Princeton, New Jersey: The Princeton Religion Research Center, 1996), 19.
5. Tom Morganthen, "The Lull Before the Storm," *Newsweek Magazine,* 4 December 1995.
6. *World Almanac,* (Funk and Wagnall's Corporation, 1995).
7. George Gallup, Jr., "Religion in America . . . 1996", 19.
8. Tom Morganthen, "The Lull Before the Storm."
9. Ibid.
10. George Gallup, Jr., "Religion in America . . . 1996."
11. Ibid.
12. Lynn May, *The Auburn Plainsman,* 23 January 1997.
13. Infopedia 2.0, Softkey International, Inc., Cambridge, Mass.
14. Tim Friend, "Heroin Spreads Across the USA," *USA Today,* 1 April 1997.
15. Snapshot, "The nation's couch potatoes," Infopedia 2.0.
16. Snapshot, "Do you know where your dating teenager is?" Infopedia 2.0.

17. Snapshot, "Happily Ever After?" *USA Today*, 6 December 1995.
18. Elmer Dewitt, Philip. "On a Screen Near You: Cyberporn," *Time* Magazine, 3 July 1995.
19. Ibid.

## OTHER BOOKS BY STEPHEN HILL:

### TIME TO WEEP

Speaks of the foundations of revival.

### WHITE CANE RELIGION
*and other messages from the Brownsville Revival*

Can the blind lead the blind?

### THE GOD MOCKERS
*and other messages from the Brownsville Revival*

Do not be deceived. God is not mocked.

### STONE-COLD HEART

Powerful testimony of Stephen Hill.

### HOT FROM THE PREACHER'S MOUND

A treasury of insights for practical Christian living.

### ON EARTH AS IT IS IN HEAVEN

Perpetual daily devotional guide. Bible reading portions by Robert Murray McCheyne, along with daily quotes from great historic preachers.